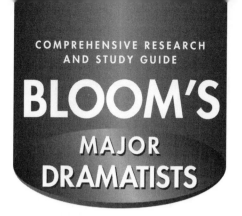

COMPREHENSIVE RESEARCH
AND STUDY GUIDE

BLOOM'S
MAJOR
DRAMATISTS

Euripides

EDITED AND WITH AN
INTRODUCTION BY HAROLD BLOOM

BLOOM'S
MAJOR DRAMATISTS

Aeschylus
Aristophanes
Bertolt Brecht
Anton Chekhov
Euripides
Henrik Ibsen
Eugène Ionesco
Ben Jonson
Christopher Marlowe
Arthur Miller
Molière
Eugene O'Neill
Luigi Pirandello
Shakespeare's Comedies
Shakespeare's Histories
Shakespeare's Romances
Shakespeare's Tragedies
George Bernard Shaw
Sam Shepard
Neil Simon
Tom Stoppard
Sophocles
Oscar Wilde
Thornton Wilder
Tennessee Williams
August Wilson

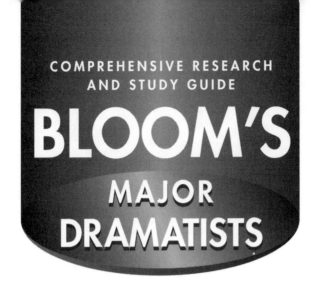

COMPREHENSIVE RESEARCH
AND STUDY GUIDE

BLOOM'S

MAJOR
DRAMATISTS

Euripides

EDITED AND WITH AN INTRODUCTION
BY HAROLD BLOOM

CHELSEA HOUSE
PUBLISHERS
A Haights Cross Communications Company

Philadelphia

A Haights Cross Communications ⟋ Company

Printed and bound in the United States of America.

First Printing
1 3 5 7 9 8 6 4 2

Library of Congress Cataloging-in-Publication Data
Euripides / edited and with an introduction by Harold Bloom.
    p. cm. — (Bloom's major dramatists)
Includes bibliographical references and index.
  ISBN 0-7910-6356-9
  1. Euripides—Criticism and interpretation. 2. Mythology, Greek, in
literature. 3. Tragedy. I. Bloom, Harold. II. Series.
  PA3978 .E88 2002
  882'.01—dc21
                        2002012360

Chelsea House Publishers
1974 Sproul Road, Suite 400
Broomall, PA 19008-0914

www.chelseahouse.com

Contributing Editor: Anne Marie Albertazzi

Produced by www.book*designing*.com

Cover design: Robert Gerson

Contents

User's Guide

This volume is designed to present biographical, critical, and bibliographical information on the author's best-known or most important works. Following Harold Bloom's editor's note and introduction is a detailed biography of the author, discussing major life events and important literary accomplishments. A plot summary of each play follows, tracing significant themes, patterns, and motifs in the work.

A selection of critical extracts, derived from previously published material from leading critics, analyzes aspects of each play. The extracts consist of statements from the author, if available, early reviews of the work, and later evaluations up to the present. A bibliography of the author's writings (including a complete list of all works written, cowritten, edited, and translated), a list of additional books and articles on the author and his or her work, and an index of themes and ideas in the author's writings conclude the volume.

～

Harold Bloom is Sterling Professor of the Humanities at Yale University and Henry W. and Albert A. Berg Professor of English at the New York University Graduate School. He is the author of over 20 books, including *Shelley's Mythmaking* (1959), *The Visionary Company* (1961), *Blake's Apocalypse* (1963), *Yeats* (1970), *A Map of Misreading* (1975), *Kabbalah and Criticism* (1975), *Agon: Toward a Theory of Revisionism* (1982), *The American Religion* (1992), *The Western Canon* (1994), and *Omens of Millennium: The Gnosis of Angels, Dreams, and Resurrection* (1996). *The Anxiety of Influence* (1973) sets forth Professor Bloom's provocative theory of the literary relationships between the great writers and their predecessors. His most recent books include *Shakespeare: The Invention of the Human,* a 1998 National Book Award finalist, and *How to Read and Why,* which was published in 2000.

Professor Bloom earned his Ph.D. from Yale University in 1955 and has served on the Yale faculty since then. He is a 1985 MacArthur Foundation Award recipient, served as the Charles Eliot Norton Professor of Poetry at Harvard University in 1987–88, and has received honorary degrees from the universities of Rome and Bologna. In 1999, Professor Bloom received the prestigious American Academy of Arts and Letters Gold Medal for Criticism.

Currently, Harold Bloom is the editor of numerous Chelsea House volumes of literary criticism, including the series BLOOM'S NOTES, BLOOM'S MAJOR DRAMATISTS, BLOOM'S MAJOR NOVELISTS, MAJOR LITERARY CHARACTERS, BLOOM'S MODERN CRITICAL VIEWS, BLOOM'S MODERN CRITICAL INTERPRETATIONS, and WOMEN WRITERS OF ENGLISH AND THEIR WORKS.

Editor's Note

My Introduction, on *The Bacchae,* centers upon the play's ambivalences, which work so as to remove both the Dionysian god and the victim-tyrant Pentheus from our sympathies. I argue that tragic irony is dominant in the play, severely qualifying Euripidean humanism.

On *Alcestis,* all the critics emphasize moral ambiguities, with Philip Vellacott seeing Euripides as a skeptic in regard to marriage, while Nicole Loraux wonders if Euripidean Tragedy can sustain "feminine glory."

The Bacchae is illuminated by William Sale's fascinating psychoanalysis of Pentheus, after which Charles Segal explores tragic paradoxes and Mary R. Lefkowitz argues that Euripides, despite the slander of him by Aristophanes, was a traditionalist on the question of the power of the gods.

Bernard Knox brilliantly apprehends the preternatural elements in Medea's character, while Bernd Seidensticker sees her as essentially masculine.

For Gilbert Murray, *Iphigeneia at Aulis* is a crucial turn in Greek drama, after which Helene P. Foley uncovers the curious dialectic of marriage and sacrifice in the play.

Introduction

HAROLD BLOOM

E. R. Dodds, in his splendid edition of the *Bacchae* (1944, 1960), explains not only the nature of Dionysiac religion, but remarks also the particular place of the play in the work of Euripides. The poet, over seventy, left Athens for Macedonia in 408 B.C.E., and never returned, dying in the winter of 407–406. In abandoning Athens, Euripides may well have felt defeated by public taste and poetic satirists. At least he did not have to endure the *Frogs* of Aristophanes, presented in Athens the year after his death. In the *Frogs*, Dionysus goes down into Hades in order to bring back a tragic poet-playwright, severely lacking in Athens after the death of the three great figures: Aeschylus, Sophocles, Euripides. Poor Euripides is savaged by Aristophanes, though nowhere near so viciously as Socrates was debased in the *Clouds*.

Dodds, still the authority upon the Greeks and the irrational, reads the *Bacchae* as being beyond any single stance by Euripides upon the Dionysiac. Euripides presents Dionysus as soft and sinister, a fatal androgyne of a god. Pentheus, the god's destined victim, also receives an equivocal representation. Neither the god nor the tyrant moves our sympathy as audience or readers.

The *Bacchae* was not presented in Athens until after the death of Euripides. We do not have a complete text of the play, but what is missing is not necessarily central. In the Hellenistic period and in Rome, the *Bacchae* was very popular, and still seems the masterpiece of Euripides' nineteen extant tragedies. William Arrowsmith, whose turbulent, wonderful translation I will employ here, compares the *Bacchae* in eminence to Sophocles's *Oedipus Tyrannus* and Aeschylus' *Agamemnon*. Like those plays, the *Bacchae* makes us into what Shakespeare called "wonder-wounded hearers." Oedipus and Clytemnestra find their rival in Euripides' uncanny Dionysus, who is a triumph of representation: disturbing, fascinating, ultimately terrifying.

Dionysiac worship came late to Hellas, and did not attempt to supplant the Olympian pantheon. In Hellenistic Alexandria and in Rome, Dionysus became Bacchus the wine-god, but in earlier Hellas he was a more comprehensive divinity, emblematic of natural abundance, of flowering life, the Power in the tree. The Maenads in the *Bacchae* have drunk no wine (Pentheus is wrong about this) but are ecstatic through mountain-dancing, a shamanistic practice, restricted in Hellas to women's societies, and still carried on by certain groups of women in the United States today. Dodds is eloquent on Dionysiac dance:

> ... he is the cause of madness and the liberator from madness ... To resist Dionysus is to repress the elemental in one's own nature; the punishment is the sudden complete collapse ... when the elemental breaks through ...

This Dionysiac dance of enthusiastic women culminated in a *sparagmos*, in which an animal body was torn apart and devoured raw, thus repeating the Titanic act of rending and consuming the infant Dionysus. The women who destroy Pentheus think he is a lion; more usually the Bacchantes ripped asunder and ate a bull, whose innate strength of resistance testifies to the daemonic ferocity imparted by Dionysus to his Maenads. There is some evidence of human sacrifice and ritual murder associated with Dionysiac celebration in the classical world. The Bacchantes achieved both the vitality of animal life and the group ecstasy in which individual consciousness vanished, for a time.

The origins of this shamanism may have been in Thrace, but in any rate it was tamed in Hellas, until the dark times of the Peloponnesian War, when it returned under the name of various mystery gods: Attis, Adonis, and Sabazius, to be deprecated and attacked by Plato, among others.

Dodds categorizes the *Bacchae* as the most severely formalized of Euripides' plays, and warns us against seeing it either as an exaltation of Dionysus or as an enlightened protest against orgiastic religions, since Pentheus is very hard to like, and Dionysus is absolutely beyond human moral categories. There is a renewed force in the aged, self-exiled Euripides of the *Bacchae*, but it is neither Dionysiac nor counter-Dionysiac. Euripides, at the end, perfected his own art as poet-dramatist. It is as though he answered his enemy Aristophanes in advance, by demonstrating that, in his own way, he could raise himself to the Sublime measure of Sophocles and of Aeschylus.

William Arrowsmith was a great humanist, who died in 1992, fighting heroically against the tides of Resentment that since have totally drowned humanism in the universities of the English-speaking world. I mourn him still, as we were close friends, and he restored my spirits, each time we met. A lover of both Euripides and Aristophanes, he refrained from translating the *Frogs,* while giving us superb version of the *Birds* and the *Clouds,* and of the *Bacchae* and four other tragedies by Euripides. Arrowsmith saw in the *Bacchae,* as in *Hippolytus* and in *Heracles,* an unique Euripidean compassion: "the pity that is born from shared suffering." To Arrowsmith, this was Euripidean humanism: "that faith and that fate which, in Euripides, makes man human, not mere god." Whether Arrowsmith, in his moral generosity and genial humaneness, imparted his own qualities to Euripides seems to me something of a question. Here is the close of the play, in Arrowsmith's version:

AGAVE

I pity you, Father.

CADMUS

And I pity you, my child,
and I grieve for your poor sisters. I pity them.

AGAVE

Terribly has Dionysus brought
disaster down upon this house.

DIONYSUS

I was terribly blasphemed,
my name dishonored in Thebes.

AGAVE

Farewell, Father.

CADMUS

Farewell to you, unhappy child.
Fare well. But you shall find your faring hard.

(*Exit Cadmus*)

AGAVE

Lead me, guides, where my sisters wait,
poor sisters of my exile. Let me go
where I shall never see Cithaeron more,
where that accursed hill may not see me,

where I shall find no trace of thyrsus!
> That I leave to other Bacchae.

> > (*Exit Agave with attendants.*)

CHORUS

> The gods have many shapes.
> The gods bring many things
> to their accomplishment.
> And what was most expected
> has not been accomplished.
> But god has found his way
> for what no man expected.
> > So ends the play.

I hear ironies that are far stronger than the traumatized pity exchanged by Cadmus and his daughter Agave, who has led the Bacchantes in slaying her own son, Pentheus. Were I a director, I would be at a loss to tell the actor playing Dionysus how to speak his frightening lines: perhaps tonelessly, or at least matter-of-fact? An actress can do virtually anything with the blinding irony of: "That I leave to other Bacchae." Since the chorus are Asian Maenads, they are no problem: their tone is triumphant, if no longer ecstatic. Tragic irony is stronger in Euripides than is any humanism. If Aristophanes attended the *Bacchae*, he would have had his view of Euripidean nihilism confirmed. But that is what I find most Shakespearean about Euripides, whose own uncanniness somehow gets into the Shakespeare of *Troilus and Cressida*. ❀

Biography of
Euripides

Euripides was the youngest of the three great ancient Greek tragic poets. The other two were Aeschylus, the oldest, and Sophocles, a contemporary of Euripides who was often his opponent in dramatic competitions. Euripides' plays, like those of Aeschylus and Sophocles, dramatize the Greek myths; in fact, they are one of the most important sources we have for knowledge of ancient Greek mythology.

Euripides was born in 484 B.C. in Athens, Greece. He is assumed to have come from a noble family, since it is recorded quite reliably that as a boy he served as a torchbearer in a festival in honor of Apollo Zosterios and poured wine for young noblemen. Euripides' growth into maturity and artistic renown coincided with the 50-year rise of democratic Athens to its political and cultural ascendancy in Greece. In 480, when he was a boy, the second Persian invasion against Greece was defeated. Following that, the Athenian empire grew in power and stature, and as Euripides reached his prime years, so did Athens, gaining great intellectual and cultural prominence in the 460s and 450s. While there is no reliable information about whom Euripides studied with, Edith Hall notes that "Euripides, intellectually, was a child of his time. Every significant field studied by the professional intellectuals ('sophists') in contemporary Athens surfaces in his tragedies: ontology, epistemology, philosophy of language, moral and political theory, medicine, psychology, and cosmology" (*Euripides* xiv).

By 440, Athens was under scrutiny by other city states for jeopardizing the very freedom she originally fought for, and in 431, the Peloponnesian War broke out, in which Sparta and other Greek city states battled with Athens over control of the Aegean. By 412, Athens' empire was crippled and her resources depleted, following the loss of a fleet and many thousands of men at Syracuse in Sicily. In 404, Athens had been completely defeated, and Euripides had gone into self-imposed exile in Macedon to die in 406, two years earlier.

It was during Athens' long struggle before her defeat that Euripides wrote the majority of his plays. Scholars' knowledge of

Euripides' dramatic output owes mostly to the Alexandrian poets who lived around 250 B.C. The Alexandrians took their name from Alexandria, Egypt, which had become the new center of Greek literature. They compiled lists of plays, including those that no longer existed, for the three tragedians. In total, they had record of 92 plays by Euripides, 78 of which they actually possessed. Today only seventeen plays of Euripides exist. The play *Rhesus* is sometimes attributed to Euripides, but was probably not written by him.

Euripides began his career as a tragic poet at age 29, three years after he saw Aeschylus' *Oresteian Trilogy* and seven years after a radical democracy was established in Athens. His dramas were performed at tragic competitions during the annual festival of Dionysus, the god of wine. This festival was held in the spring, when the vine first put forth its branches, and all business ceased for several days. People gathered to watch great plays, and writers such as Euripides were considered to be in the service of the god himself. There was a sense that Dionysus himself was present, and it was believed that performing and watching the Plays was tantamount to reverent worship.

Euripides won the first prize five times, three times for plays that are still extant: *Hippolytus, Iphigeneia at Aulis,* and *Bacchae. Hippolytus* was performed in 428, two years after an outbreak of plague in Athens, and *Iphigeneia at Aulis* and *Bacchae* were performed posthumously, coinciding with the defeat of Athens by Sparta in the Peloponnesian War. *Alcestis* (ca. 438) won second prize, followed by *Medea* (431), which won third prize and coincided with the eruption of war between Athens and Sparta. Next came *Children of Heracles* (ca. 430), *Andromache* (ca. 425), *Hecuba* (ca. 424), *Suppliant Women* (ca. 423) and *Electra* (ca. 420). *Heracles* (ca. 416) and *Trojan Women* (415, second prize) were produced during the desperate time in which Athens slaughtered the men of the island of Melos and enslaved their women and children. *Iphigeneia among the Taurians* (ca. 414), *Ion* (ca. 413), *Helen* (412), and *Cyclops* (satyr play, ca. 412) followed soon after Athens' ill-fated attempt to capture Sicily and the loss of her fleet, and *Phoenician Women* (ca. 410, second prize) and *Orestes* (408) came after the dissolution of the radical democracy in Athens in favor of a Spartan-led oligarchy.

The fact that these tumultuous events coincided with the production of Euripides' dramas leads many critics to focus on the nearly ubiquitous presence of irony in Euripides' works. Much of the literary scholarship on these works examines to a considerable degree, and with varied perspectives, the extent to which this irony represents an irreverent or cynical attitude toward the conventions surrounding ancient Greek institutions such as marriage, religion, and war. Some of the information about Euripides comes from extant works of Aristophanes, whose comedies portray Euripides as lyrically decadent, religiously unorthodox, and shockingly immoral. Though this comic treatment of Euripides may not be fact, it contains an element of truth, as reflected by Edith Hall's comment on *Medea:* "The play must have been ethically shocking. The vengeful, competitive, and sexually honest Medea, in escaping unpunished, was any Athenian husband's worst nightmare realized" (*Euripides* xvi). While Euripides used traditional themes, such as the fragility of life and the complex relationship between humans and the gods, his ironic perspective on those themes questioned traditional attitudes toward them, and continue to do so today. ❀

Plot Summary of
Alcestis

Alcestis presents two characters, Admetus and Alcestis, who escape death in different ways: Admetus does so by staying one step ahead of it, while Alcestis does so by surrendering to it. As Philip Vellacott has written, "The theme of *Alcestis* is the inexorable power of Necessity . . . and the story presents this theme in two aspects: the absolute impact of death, and the insoluble dilemma of marriage" (Introduction to *Euripides: Three Plays* 16). Euripides treats the theme of necessity ironically, as Admetus does not want to die until he has escaped death, and Alcestis is not allowed to continue her life until she has embraced death. In ancient Greek culture, a woman's life was considered less valuable than a man's, and her marriage to him was her assent to give her life to him. Euripides' play, which highlights the irony of what happens when the marriage contract is taken to its furthest and most literal implications, can be seen as either a judgment against the harsh inequality of marriage in his time or a celebration of the heroism that the marriage contract is capable of producing.

The action takes place in front of the palace of Admetus at Pherae in Thessaly. Apollo enters from the palace and delivers a prologue in which he reviews the events that have led up to the present, foretells the future, and provides a thematic context. Apollo and his son Asclepius rebelled against Zeus: Asclepius used medicine to raise the dead, thus flouting the distinction between mortals and gods, and when Zeus killed Asclepius Apollo retaliated by killing Zeus' workmen, the Cyclopes. In retaliation, Zeus sentenced Apollo to a term of servitude to a mortal, Admetus of Pherae. In gratitude for his former master's beneficence, Apollo has freed Admetus from his fated early death by tricking the Fates and getting them to agree to accept another mortal's death instead. The only person Admetus could find to stand in for him in death is his wife Alcestis. She is now close to death.

Apollo sees Death approaching, preparing to take Alcestis to Hades, or the underworld. He asks Death if there is any way Alcestis can be spared, but Death forbids it, as he takes pleasure in his work. Apollo presages that Death will be defeated in this quest by a man who is coming to the palace on his way to capture the man-eating mares of Diomedes for Eurystheus. Here he is referring to Heracles (Hercules), who in penance for killing his family was instructed by the oracle at Delphi to perform the Twelve Labors for Eurystheus, king of Mycenae. Apollo reveals to Death that Heracles will be entertained as a guest of Admetus and "take the woman from you by force." Thus, Alcestis will ultimately be saved. Death shrugs off Apollo's threat and enters the palace to collect Alcestis.

The chorus expresses worry and grief over the imminent death of so great and noble a lady and wishes Apollo's son Asclepius were still alive to raise her from the dead. A maidservant enters from the palace and relates to a curious chorus that Alcestis is on the verge of death, "both living and dead," a phrase that ironically signifies her imminent shift of fate. The maidservant tells the chorus that her mistress was prayerful and noble in preparing herself for death, and wept uncontrollably when she bade farewell to her marriage bed. Admetus weeps for her inside, begging her not to leave him as she lies in his arms. As Alcestis, Admetus, and their two children enter from the palace, the chorus leader concludes "I shall never henceforth say that marriage causes more joy than pain."

Alcestis tells her husband that she chose to die because it would be better that he lived with the children and the family remained intact, than if she lived without him at the mercy of a new man who would put his children above hers. She laments that Admetus' father did not offer his life instead, since that would have been a highly noble act. By dying for his son, he would have allowed the young married couple to live out their life rather than hang on to his aged life. Alcestis' final request to Admetus is that he never marry again, thus sparing her children from an uncaring stepmother. Admetus promises he will not marry and in addition swears to never stop mourning, to live celibately, and to experience pleasure only when he embraces her memorial statue. Alcestis dies, leaving her devastated child to proclaim that "the house is utterly destroyed." The chorus laments bitterly at the loss of so great a woman, expressing their undying loyalty to her, "For you, you alone, dear among women, had the courage to redeem your husband from Hades at the price of your life."

Heracles enters from the entrance that leads from the countryside. He tells the chorus that he is on his way to capture Diomedes' man-eating horses for the lord of Tiryns (Eurystheus); but the chorus warns him that both the horses and their owner are ferocious and the task may be lethal. When Heracles sees Admetus enter in mourning clothes he becomes concerned and moves to leave, but Admetus, in order to be a proper host, covers up the fact that his wife has died and claims he merely mourns the death of a family friend. Admetus insists Heracles stay, despite Heracles' offer to stay with another friend. The chorus calls Admetus foolish, but Admetus explains that Heracles has always been a generous host to him and "my house does not know how to reject or dishonor guests." There is some ambiguity as to whether Admetus is being an honorable and magnanimous host or whether he is motivated by a superficial concern for his reputation.

Later, Admetus returns, followed by servants who carry the body of Alcestis on a bier. His father Pheres, former king, arrives to pay respects and offer finery, but Admetus rejects him, complaining that Pheres was selfish not to offer his life for his son, causing Alcestis to sacrifice herself. Pheres, offended, refuses to accept any responsibility for Alcestis' death and calls Admetus a coward for letting his wife die in place of him. Despite the chorus' pleading that they stop arguing, Admetus and his father continue to bicker, each concluding the other is shameless and mean. Pheres leaves and Admetus exits with the funeral procession.

A manservant enters onto an empty stage, complaining of Heracles' abominable drunken behavior. He is indignant that he and the other servants are forbidden by Admetus to show no signs of grief while they serve Heracles' every drunken whim, and that their work prevents them from paying respects to the woman whom they regard as a mother. Heracles enters, criticizing the manservant for being overly morose over an insignificant death, leading the manservant to reveal to him that it was Alcestis who died. Heracles, hearing that Admetus hid her death in order to be a generous host, is touched. He asks where Alcestis' tomb is, determined to show his gratitude to his host by doing battle with Death and bringing Alcestis back from the dead.

After the manservant and Heracles part ways, Admetus enters with the funeral procession and in his grief wishes for death, since life without his wife is now meaningless. The irony here is that his wish to avoid death caused his present situation, and his escape from death has now devalued his life. The chorus tries to console him by saying that his wife's love still remains, and many men before him have lost their wives. Admetus is penitent, fully aware of the disgrace that his actions have caused. The chorus observes that Admetus is caught in the "ineluctable chains" of the goddess Necessity, a metaphorical lady who has no statues, no altars, and heeds no sacrifice.

Heracles enters with a veiled woman. He pretends to be angry at Admetus for not speaking frankly to him about his wife's death. He asks Admetus to keep the veiled woman for him while he goes on his pursuit of Diomedes' mares. He suggests to Admetus that a new union with another woman will soothe his grief. Admetus refuses, horrified at the thought of bringing another woman into his house; she will be a constant reminder of his wife and cause him bitter grief. At this point he proves his loyalty to his wife, since his decision is made supposedly in his wife's absence. Hercules forces a reluctant Admetus to take the woman's hand, and Admetus does so with his head turned away. Then Hercules throws back the woman's veil to reveal Alcestis, whom he has brought back from the dead.

Admetus rejoices, calling himself "blessed by fortune." The chorus concludes the play with the Euripidean stock ending, which says that the gods' accomplishments are always different than expected, so it is wise not to be confident in any expectation. ❀

List of Characters in
Alcestis

Apollo is the mythical god of light, truth, music, healing, prophecy, and manly beauty. He and his son Asclepius rebelled against Zeus, so Zeus sentenced Apollo to a term of servitude to a mortal, Admetus of Pherae. In gratitude for his former master's beneficence, Apollo has freed Admetus from his fated early death by tricking the Fates and getting them to agree to accept another mortal's death instead. Apollo gives the opening speech of the play and tells this story. When Apollo asks Death to spare Alcestis' life, Death refuses, but Apollo predicts Heracles' confrontation with death and rescue of Alcestis, thus foreshadowing the conclusion of the play.

Death is a mythological god who dwells in the underworld. He arrives at the house of Admetus to carry away Alcestis, who has agreed to die in place of her husband. When Apollo asks him to spare Alcestis, he refuses and reminds him that he enjoys his occupation. Death's stubbornness introduces the theme of Necessity; death is absolute and will not accept bargaining.

The Chorus are men of Pherae. They are sympathetic to Alcestis, proclaiming their loyalty to her and lamenting her predicament in this marriage. Their grief may be interpreted as Euripides' judgment of the harsh inequalities inherent in marriage.

The Maidservant functions both as a messenger who describes action offstage and a grieving devotee of Alcestis who creates sympathy for her. She tells the chorus of Alcestis' farewell to her bedchamber before her death; Alcestis is tearful and inconsolable as she contemplates that she will never sleep in the bed with her husband again.

Alcestis is the wife of Admetus, king of Pherae. She agrees to die for Admetus, who has been told he will escape death if another mortal dies in his place. Her uncomplaining self-sacrifice makes her the ideal wife in a sense; she reasons that the family structure would survive much better if she died rather than her husband. Ironically, such a wife is no good to Admetus, who is practically dead with grief after she dies. Alcestis is taken back from the underworld by Heracles, who presents her to Admetus disguised behind a veil. When Alcestis' identity is revealed, Heracles tells Admetus that he will not be able to hear her speak for three days. Alcestis ultimately is rewarded for her willingness to die for her husband.

Admetus is the king of Pherae, husband of Alcestis, and former master of Apollo. Apollo helps Admetus escape death by getting the Fates to accept the death of another mortal in his place. When we first see Admetus he is saying goodbye to his wife, who has agreed to die for him. As he continues to grieve, he becomes more and more remorseful, realizing that the life he has without her is no use living. Admetus' hospitality towards Heracles, in spite of his wife's death, impresses his guest, so Heracles takes Alcestis back from the underworld. Ironically, it is only when Admetus refuses to accept a disguised Alcestis into his house that Heracles allows him to see that the woman in disguise is his wife. Admetus' fate, subject to the goddess Necessity, exemplifies the common Euripidean theme of the unpredictability of life under the whims of the gods.

The Child is the son of Admetus and Alcestis. His grief over the loss of his mother, in which he laments that her death renders the house "utterly destroyed," is ironic in that his mother's does not threaten the integrity of the family structure in the way his father's death would. The child's bitterness over being left an orphan is one of the tragic moments in the play that evokes the audience's pity.

Heracles is known as the greatest hero of Greek mythology. When he appears in the play, he is on his way to completing one of the many labors that Eurystheus, king of Mycenae, has assigned to him as a penance for killing his children. Heracles happens to visit Admetus on the day Alcestis dies, but Admetus covers up the fact that his wife has died so he can be a proper host to Heracles. When Heracles finds out, he is in the midst of drunken revelry but manages to gather his wits. He is so impressed by Admetus' unselfishness that he goes to the underworld to bring Alcestis back to her husband. Heracles' comical drunkenness provides a contrast to the tragic action of the play.

Pheres is Admetus' father and the former king. When he arrives to pay respects after Alcestis' death, Admetus accuses him of being selfish in not offering to die for him and causing Alcestis to sacrifice herself. Pheres is offended and calls Admetus a coward for letting his wife die in place of him. Pheres' refusal to make such a sacrifice for his son can be seen as fatherly and wise, or perhaps as a reinforcement that in this play, self-sacrifice is ultimately a feminine role.

The Manservant is one of Admetus' servants. While Heracles is carousing, he enters onto an empty stage and complains of Heracles' abominable drunken behavior. His loyalty to Alcestis, against Admetus, reinforces her saintliness: he is indignant at being forbidden by Admetus to grieve and angry that his work prevents him from paying respects to the woman whom he regards as a mother. When Heracles comes out to criticize the manservant for being overly morose, the manservant reveals to him that Alcestis has died. The manservant functions as a messenger of sorts, as well as providing humor and sympathy. ✿

Critical Views on
Alcestis

[Gilbert Murray (1866–1957) was the regius professor of Greek at Oxford and translator of numerous Greek authors, including Euripides, Aeschylus, Sophocles and Aristophanes. His books include *History of Ancient Greek Literature* (1897), *The Rise of the Greek Epic* (1907), *The Classical Tradition in Poetry* (1927), and *Hellenism and the Modern World* (1953). In this excerpt from the introduction to his translation of the play, Murray shows that *Alcestis* is a clear example of the Pro-satyric form.]

Now we are of late years beginning to understand much better what a Satyr-play was. Satyrs have, of course, nothing to do with satire, either etymologically or otherwise. Satyrs are the attendant daemons who form the Kômos, or revel rout, of Dionysus. They are represented in divers fantastic forms, the human or divine being mixed with that of some animal, especially the horse or wild goat. Like Dionysus himself, they are connected in ancient religion with the Renewal of the Earth in spring and the resurrection of the dead, a point which students of the *Alcestis* may well remember. But in general they represent mere joyous creatures of nature, unthwarted by law and unchecked by self-control. Two notes are especially struck by them: the passions and the absurdity of half-drunken revellers, and the joy and mystery of the wild things in the forest.

The rule was that after three tragedies proper there came a play, still in tragic diction, with a traditional saga plot and heroic characters, in which the Chorus was formed by these Satyrs. There was a deliberate clash, an effect of burlesque; but of course the clash must not be too brutal. Certain characters of the heroic saga are, so to speak, at home with Satyrs and others are not. To take our extant specimens of Satyr-plays, for instance: in the *Cyclops* we have Odysseus, the heroic trickster; in the fragmentary *Ichneutae* of Sophocles we have the Nymph Cyllene, hiding the baby Hermes from the chorus by the most barefaced and pleasant lying; later no doubt there was an entrance of the infant thief himself. Autolycus,

Sisyphus, Thersites are all Satyr-play heroes and congenial to the Satyr atmosphere; but the most congenial of all, the one hero who existed always in an atmosphere of Satyrs and the Kômos until Euripides made him the central figure of a tragedy, was Heracles.[1]

The complete Satyr-play had a hero of this type and a Chorus of Satyrs. But the complete type was refined away during the fifth century; and one stage in the process produced a play with a normal chorus but with one figure of the Satyric or "revelling" type. One might almost say the "comic" type if, for the moment, we may remember that that word is directly derived from 'Kômos.'

The *Alcestis* is a very clear instance of this Pro-satyric class of play. It has the regular tragic diction, marked here and there (393, 756, 780, etc.) by slight extravagances and forms of words which are sometimes epic and sometimes over-colloquial; it has a regular saga plot, which had already been treated by the old poet Phrynichus in his *Alcestis,* a play which is now lost but seems to have been Satyric; and it has one character straight from the Satyr world, the heroic reveller, Heracles. It is all in keeping that he should arrive tired, should feast and drink and sing; should be suddenly sobered and should go forth to battle with Death. It is also in keeping that the contest should have a half-grotesque and half-ghastly touch, the grapple amid the graves and the cracking ribs.

Note
[1] The character of Heracles in connexion with the Kômos, already indicated by Wilamowitz and Dieterich (*Herakles*, pp. 98, ff.; *Pulcinella*, pp. 63, ff.), has been illuminatingly developed in an unpublished monograph by Mr. J. A. K. Thomson, of Aberdeen.

—Gilbert Murray, *The Alcestis of Euripides* (New York: Oxford University Press, 1915): pp. vii–ix.

ANNE PIPPIN BURNETT ON THE VIRTUES OF ADMETUS

[Anne Pippin Burnett is the author of *Catastrophe Survived: Euripides' Plays of Mixed Reversal* (1971), *Revenge in Attic and Later Tragedy* (1988), and *Three Archaic Poets: Archilochus, Alcaeus, Sappho* (1983). In this excerpt, Burnett argues that Euripides did not intend his audience to see Admetus as cowardly or punishable.]

The *Alcestis* nowadays is commonly described as a psychological drama which has as its true subject an absurd disparity between outmoded ideals and actual human conduct. It is usually said that Euripides has portrayed the noble action of a fairy-tale heroine, then capped it with ignoble consequences. Some scholars, however, turn a skeptic's eye even upon Alcestis and her sacrifice. Those who admire the queen often assert that she dies disillusioned, while the true debunkers explain that she is dying for base reasons that show her to be as false and calculating as her mate. Critics who believe in Alcestis but find her husband unworthy of her read the play as a bourgeois-realist comedy with a plot that breaks all the rules of realism. Those who find both the king and the queen to be cheap imitations of tragic nobility discover a Shavian marital fable ending with the reunion of a pair who will live unhappily ever after, each a thorn in the other's flesh. Both groups believe that the secret of the play is hypocrisy, conscious or unconscious; they argue that principals and chorus often do not mean what they say, and that Euripides meant only the simpletons in his audience to take his play at face value. These critics seem to forget, in dealing with the *Alcestis*, the enormous spatial candor of the ancient theater, and the difficulty of conveying innuendo from behind a mask.

I should like to play the simpleton, and attempt a naive reading of Euripides' *Alcestis*. The way has been prepared for many years, ever since Lesky's study of the fable's fairy-tale forms showed that the story itself makes no evaluation of the husband's acceptance of his wife's sacrifice, though it plainly condemns the parents. Euripides, then, in choosing as his *mythos* the mixed tale of the bargain with death and the love sacrifice, was not choosing a story which necessarily dealt with a cad or a coward. It was doubtless within his power to give the king these qualities if he wished, but if the conventional story of a favorite of the gods was to be given a new tone of moral corruption, the change would have to be strongly made. A straightforward dramatist would establish the altered ethical coloring of his king as soon as possible; a writer of more subtlety might lull his audience for a while, then suddenly force them to see the baseness of the man they had admired. In this case, however, the longer the revelation was postponed, the more shocking and incontrovertible it would have to be when made. Euripides, however, follows neither of these courses. His opening description of Admetus is of a king, hero, and favorite of Apollo. At the play's end the entire kingdom, the entire generation, has had its admiration of the man, his wife, and his friend, strengthened and confirmed. The audience has nowhere been instructed to separate its judgment from that of the chorus. Nor has its attention ever been directed to what must be, in a re-evaluation of the Admetus story, the crucial moment for revision: the moment when Admetus accepted his wife's offer to trade her life for his. Euripides, in fact, has gone to considerable trouble to discourage his audience from thinking of this moment at all.

In fairy tale the bargain and its fulfilment both belonged to the king's wedding day; the family refuses, the bride insists, and at once she sinks away as her dying husband is revived. Euripides has split this single action in two, making a new chronology that stretches over an indefinite length of time. No word of his text describes the circumstances of the past bargain: how Apollo announced it, how Admetus made his canvass, how Alcestis offered herself, and how Admetus received that offer. All these matters are ignored, though three passages mysteriously suggest that Admetus was virtually dead at the time (13, 462–63, 633). The bargain is stated as fact; Apollo's first (and presumably inalterable) arrangement with the Moirai in two lines (14–15), the subsequent actions of Admetus and his family in three (15–18). The only motivation discussed is that of Apollo; he sponsored the bargain as a boon for Admetus, to show his gratitude for that man's pious hospitality. Euripides' new chronology supplies one new detail, however; in his version of the bargain, the death that was offered and accepted was not an immediate death but one set vaguely in the future, allowing a certain amount of continued common life to both the receiver and the giver. This amelioration would hardly have been added by a poet bent on condemning the king.

The play allows us to watch what happened on the day the bargain was fulfilled, but places behind a veil of time the day when Alcestis made her promise to the Fates. It was Euripides, as far as we know, who made this unmeasured chasm of years appear in the middle of the old story, and the effect of the innovation is plain. The bargain assumes the unquestioned inevitability of historical event. In the course of his play the dramatist explores and evaluates Alcestis' decision by making her, on this later day, repeat her old reasons, but there is no similar exploration in the case of Admetus. He has no decision today, since her death cannot now be prevented, and the audience is not encouraged to think that he was allowed a decision on the long-ago bargain day. That bargain was engineered by Apollo and presented to Admetus in token of gratitude, and one thing Euripides has made his chorus say, at a crucial moment in the denouement, is that one must accept the gift offered by a god. ⟨. . .⟩

The visible action of the *Alcestis* represents the bargain's fulfilment, and then its remarkable dissolution. The cost is met, the article secured, then suddenly the price is returned and the purchase becomes a free gift. The audience sees Alcestis die and sees her carried out; it sees her husband take a visitor into his house and drive another away; it sees him refuse to go back into his house alone and refuse to take a strange woman in with him; then suddenly the strange woman proves to be the dead wife, and the man who bought his own life at the price of hers re-enters his house, his purchase still secure but with the price paid once more in his hands. This is the skeleton of the *Alcestis;* it acquires its flesh and form, its ugliness or beauty, from the speeches which Euripides has written for his characters. As they speak the king and queen at least must be heard with the ordinary good faith granted to all the figures who walk the classic stage, for there is nothing in the tradition, nothing in their past, and nothing in the play's overt system of rewards and punishments to suggest that this man and woman are false. If the dramatist is playing a subtle game with the material he has chosen, if in spite of the positive evaluations of the action he himself has created he means his creatures to be doubted, he will label their lies, or show a strong contradiction between their words and their accomplished deeds.

—Anne Pippin Burnett, "The Virtues of Admetus." *Classical Philology* 60, no. 4 (1965): pp. 240–42.

PHILIP VELLACOTT ON THE PLAY AS CRITIQUE OF ANCIENT MARRIAGE CUSTOMS

[Philip Vellacott has translated the plays of Aeschylus, Euripides, Menander, and Theophrastus and is the author of *Sophocles and Oedipus: A Study of* Oedipus Tyrannus, *with a New Translation* (1971) and *The Logic of Tragedy: Morals and Integrity in Aeschylus'* Oresteia (1984). In this excerpt, Vellacott contextualizes Alcestis' decision to die within the accepted conventions of ancient Greek society, and shows how Euripides' play questions those conventions.]

Why did Alcestis offer to die in place of Admetus? Her reason is first given (180) in the speech of her serving-maid who reports her words, spoken with tears to her marriage-bed: 'I am dying because I cannot bear to fail in my duty to you and to my husband.' This view of a wife's duty the chorus recognize as being an ideal which is generally accepted and thought honourable, but very rarely exemplified. It is not an ideal which Alcestis set for herself; she found it already understood by society, but she embraced it with a thoroughness which was her own rare and heroic achievement. This devotion was based not on passionate love for Admetus, but on acceptance of the ideal current in her society of what a 'house' (*oikos*) should be—an institution dedicated to the permanence of the family, to peaceful rule and stable succession. Within this framework Alcestis, being cast in heroic mould, achieves her freedom; but it is not the freedom to live. One strict measure of the freedom to live was given by Apollo to Admetus; and it enslaved him to misery and self-contempt (197–8 *et al.*).

We are now approaching an answer to the question, Why does Euripides carefully avoid mentioning the crucial moment when Admetus accepted his wife's offer? Let us consider a hypothetical answer: Because in every society known to Hellenes or to barbarians it is unquestioningly accepted that, in the broadest terms and in the last resort, woman's life is at the service and disposal of man's. Even if theoretically it was possible for Admetus to decline, yet when his wife made the offer it would actually seem to him to be above all things *right*—right in a degree beyond the achievement of most men's wives; to refuse it would seem to flout an order of nature and to annul a gesture of unique beauty. This is the attitude of the chorus of Pheraean Elders. The play assumes that the audience will not question this attitude, for in the play the only people who question it are the two slaves. It was so obvious that this self-sacrifice was the perfection of wifehood, the consummation of an ideal union. Such is the situation to which Euripides is speaking. He is not saying that this situation is wrong, nor that it is right; rather he asks, What are its effects? Sometimes this principle of the superior value of man leads to evident injustice, as in Jason's treatment of Medea or Agamemnon's of Clytemnestra and Iphigenia; and then it is clear that a principle is being abused. But here, in the earliest extant play, we are shown a good husband and a good wife, marriage at its best, suddenly faced with the *anankē* of death; and the woman loses her life but gains immortal glory, while the man keeps his life and loses everything that makes it worth keeping. The never-mentioned moment is in fact the focus of the play. This is the 'bitterness' to which W. D. Smith's essay refers; a bitterness rooted in the 'dislocation of values' which must occur when society assumes that in the last resort a woman's life is a reasonable price for a man's life. The story shows the social principle of male ascendancy, established partly by nature and partly by man's power to organize the world for his own purposes, resulting in man's shame and confusion. As a final irony, the poet ensures that this hard lesson shall not be offered to any except the few who will resolutely search for it, by presenting this piece as the fourth of a set, a recognizable substitute for a satyr-play.

The pith of the author's comment on the man–woman relationship in marriage is found in the Female Servant's description of Alcestis saying farewell to her home (170–81):

> Then she went to every altar
> In the whole palace, and before praying decked each one
> With garlands of green myrtle she had picked herself.
> No tear fell, not a sigh was heard. Her lovely face
> Did not change colour, gave no sign of what must come.
> Then, to her room; and now indeed, flinging herself
> Down on the bed, she wept. 'O marriage-bed,' she cried,
> 'Farewell! Here once I gave my maidenhood to him;
> And now my life. I do not hate you; yet you have
> Killed me, for I alone would not be false to you
> And to my husband; and for this I die.'

The contrast between the two pictures given here by the Servant is quite different from the contrast Medea spoke of, between the 'enviable life' and 'living death' which a woman might find in marriage. Medea's husband was insensitive and self-loving; Alcestis' husband is sensitive and self-critical. The case of Alcestis is in fact more tragic than Medea's; for the cause of despair is not unkindness but the accepted form of goodness. The status of Alcestis as mistress of a household, as mother of a family, is enviable, a *zēlōtos aiōn,* and the recalling of it, as she performs sacrifice at the household altars, induces no tear or sigh. But her situation as a wife, being the most enviable that any woman could hope for, has laid upon her an obligation which calls for unquenchable weeping. Neither in the Servant's narrative nor in the scene which follows does Alcestis speak of love. She 'honours' her husband (*presbeuousa,* 282; the Servant uses *protimōsa,* 155). Only the chorus in 473 use the word *philia.* The tragedy lies in the assumptions of marriage itself, which imposes an obligation without postulating its necessary motive of love. The bed which has taken her life is, in the first place, not one that she chose; Pelias gave her to Admetus, and in that she was lucky—until Admetus fell ill. In the second place the bed stands for the essence of woman's relationship to man, which is her expendability in his interest. Alcestis' tears flow not merely on her own account but on behalf of all women. The chorus agrees that for a wife to fulfil this condition of the marriage-bond is as admirable as it is rare; but no one, except the Female Slave whose narrative we are studying, doubts that it is a proper condition and that to fulfil it is miraculously right. The cost of this condition in a good marriage is spelt out in lines 183–98. Its cost in a bad marriage is left to the listener's imagination or experience.

—Philip Vellacott, *Ironic Drama: A Study of Euripides' Method and Meaning* (Cambridge: Cambridge University Press, 1975): pp. 101–3.

Justina Gregory on the Distinction Between Necessity and Free Will

[Justina Gregory has translated the fables of Aesop and is the author of *Euripides and the Instruction of the Athenians* (1991). In this excerpt, Gregory argues that Alcestis' decision to die is significant in that it reflects the eroded boundary between necessity and free will.]

With the first lines of the *Alcestis* we are given to understand that the traditional literary attributes of death have been suspended. No longer is death unpredictable, inevitable and irreversible. And although this initial situation is an inherited feature of the myth, Euripides is not content to adopt it without questioning its premises or seeking its validation. In his hands the traditional features of the story become as problematical as his own innovations.

Death, then, has become subject to variation: it is both predictable and avoidable for Admetus, predictable but unavoidable for Alcestis, and finally (although none of the mortals could have foreseen this) reversible for her. From the great leveller death is transformed into the great divider. Different characters are permitted to choose different deaths; their eligibility for death becomes a subject for debate. This alteration in the ways of death has unexpected but entirely logical results. Death is by definition the opposite of life; therefore, as death becomes differentiated, so life becomes undifferentiated. A new kind of levelling takes place: all the intentions, judgments, categories which give shape to human existence become mixed with their opposites, or with intermediary positions. The play itself may be seen as a working out of this process, and the pattern of loss of distinctions may be seen to impart a certain unity to the episodes, diverse as they may be.[17] ⟨. . .⟩

The heroine of the piece, Alcestis, is the first to suffer from the loss of distinctions, as the nature of her act is obscured even before she has carried it to its conclusion. Alcestis' self-devotion was, above all, an act of free will. In contrast to the parents who refused to die for their son, she was willing; the voluntary nature of her death constitutes her unique glory (150–155). In the course of the play, however, this supreme act of free will is also spoken of as a necessity. It is not just that sacrifice was an open choice in the past, but is one no longer. That fact would explain the references to the "destined day" of her death.[22] But it does not account for the insistence with which Euripides juxtaposes the contradictory motifs of free will and necessity; it does not account for Alcestis' remark that she has to die (320), or her reflection that "a god caused this" (298), or her final "unwilling" (389) farewell.

The contradiction has not gone unnoticed and psychological explanations have not been lacking. Alcestis, it is said, was willing to sacrifice herself once, when she still loved Admetus; now her love has cooled, and she regrets her original offer.[23] But explanations of this sort depend on assumptions about the psychology of characters who possess, after all, no independent existence outside the play.[24] The contradiction is perhaps less important for what it tells us about Alcestis than as part of a pattern of action. What has happened is that the distinction between free will and necessity has been eroded: the same event is perceived simultaneously as voluntary and involuntary, just as Alcestis is perceived simultaneously as alive and dead. This double vision has the effect of robbing Alcestis of her special glory. If making a virtue of necessity enhances many a sacrificial heroine (Polyxena in the *Hecuba,* for instance, or Iphigenia in the *IA*), making a necessity of virtue can only have the opposite result.

Notes

[17] My discussion of the "pattern of loss of distinctions" is much influenced by RENÉ GIRARD'S La Violence et le Sacré, Paris 1972, 77 ff. and passim. GIRARD defines cultural differentiation as an essential ordering mechanism in society:

"*Degrée, gradus,* est le principe de tout ordre naturel et culturel. C'est lui qui permet de situer les êtres les uns par rapport aux autres, qui fait que les choses ont un sense au sein d'un tout organisé et hiérarchisé. C'est lui qui constitue les objects et les valeurs que les hommes transforment, échangent et manipulent" (78).

[22] See DALE XVI and ANDRÉ RIVIER, En marge d'Alceste et de quelques interprétations récentes, Mus. Hel. 29, 1972, 128.

[23] This theory has its origins in the discussion by WILAMOWITZ (Griechische Tragödien III, 87). It is further elaborated by VON FRITZ 275–276; 304–305 and by E. R. SCHWINGE, Die Stellung der Trachinierinnen im Werk des Sophokles, Göttingen 1962, 42–69, and: Zwei sprachliche Bemerkungen zu Euripides' Alkestis, Glotta 48, 1970, 36–39.

[24] Cf. the refutation of VON FRITZ by LESKY 285–286, of SCHWINGE by RIVIER (above n. 22, 133–134; 137–138).

—Justina Gregory, "Euripides' *Alcestis.*" *Hermes* 107 (1979): pp. 261–62, 263–64.

NICOLE LORAUX ON THE AMBIGUOUS NATURE OF FEMININE GLORY IN TRAGEDY

[Nicole Loraux's many works include *The Children of Athena: Athenian Ideas About Citizenship and the Division Between the Sexes* (1981; translated from the French by Caroline Levine, 1993) and *Born of the Earth: Myth and Politics in Athens* (translated from the French by Selina Stewart, 2000), and she is the coeditor of *Antiquities* (2001). In this excerpt, Loraux examines the ambiguity surrounding Alcestis' fulfillment of marriage through death.]

The time has come to bring out what tragedy's treatment of the death of women borrows from socially accepted norms in classical Athens, and what separates it from them. What is at stake is the thorny question of the "glory of women"; even the most routine formulation of this is not entirely covered by Pericles' terse declaration.

The funerary epitaphs, which represent a traditional ethic, are not so uncompromising, where women's glory is concerned, as the radicalism of Pericles in his funeral speech. The idea is not completely strange to them, but this glory, which is always subordinated to a career as a "good wife," often merges into feminine "worth." This means that the glory of women is often mentioned in a tentative, not to say reticent, manner. Female worth is never confused with real worth, which belongs to men and in their case needs no further specification. There is no male worth, there is simply *aretē* itself.

Listen to the words of mourning in their orthodox form:

> Supposing that feminine virtue still exists in the human race, she partook of it

cautiously says an epitaph from Amorgos; and an inscription from the Piraeus goes further:

> Glykera was found to have a double gift, which is rare in women's nature—virtue allied to chastity.

In the praise and admiration of mankind that are sometimes accorded to a wife, her death, that final accident, counts for nothing and the life she led for everything. This is the sentiment in another epitaph from the Piraeus:

> What is in the world the highest praise for a woman
> Chairippe received in the fullest measure, when she died.

Still more explicit is the epitaph engraved on the tomb of an Athenian woman:

> It was you, Anthippe, who in the world had the most
> acclaim open to women. Now that you are dead, you have
> it still.

So much for the daily glory of women. This may have been, for Athens, substantial, but it is also very little. It is true that "good" wives are not material for tragedy.

This does not mean that women in tragedy are not wives. But they are wives in their deaths—and apparently only in their deaths, because only their deaths belong to them, and in them they bring their marriages to fulfillment. It follows that we can take two views of their deaths, contradictory but at the same time complementary. The first, which is attuned to traditional values, holds that in fulfilling themselves as spouses in their deaths the heroines of tragedy are confirming tradition at the very moment that they are innovating. The second view, which is anxious to lay hold of anything in tragedy that tends to support the "women's side," takes the point that wives in death win a renown that goes far beyond the praise traditionally granted to their sex. It is not necessary to choose one view over the other: each has its truth, and in fact it is impossible not to accept, in each case, both at once. This is what is meant by ambiguity, and there must have been an ambiguous thrill to the *katharsis* when, during a tragic performance, male citizens watched with emotion the suffering of these heroic women, represented onstage by other male citizens dressed in women's clothes. Women's glory in tragedy was an ambiguous glory.

Take the case of Alcestis, an exemplary figure in this interpretation of marriage through death. The chorus readily says of her that "of all women she behaved the best toward her husband." Her last word is to say to her husband "farewell" (*chaire*), just like those fair effigies on the stelae in Athenian cemeteries. And yet this irreproachable figure of Alcestis strikingly shows the way in which the glory of women is always twisted. Alcestis was devoted, loving, and virtuous, but she earned her "glorious death" only through the male qualities of courage and endurance. Since a fine death is essentially virile and the loyal wife has taken the man's place, this *tolma* has the recoil effect of feminizing the well-loved husband. He is driven to become the mother as well as the father of their children, and condemned to live henceforward cloistered like a virgin or chaste as a bride inside the palace, which his wife has left to join in death the open spaces of manly heroism.

—Nicole Loraux, *Tragic Ways of Killing a Woman*, trans. Anthony Forster (Cambridge, Mass.: Harvard University Press, 1987): pp. 26–29.

ROBERT C. KETTERER ON THE STATUE MOTIF

[Robert C. Ketterer's work on classical literature has been published in *Renaissance Studies, Comparative Drama,* and *Music & Letters.* In this excerpt, Ketterer examines the significance of Alcestis' statuesque appearance at the end of the play, comparing it to the statue motifs in Shakespeare's *The Winter's Tale* and Puccini's opera *Suor Angelica.*]

The statue motif appears early in this play. As Alcestis is dying in front of Admetus' eyes, he promises never to marry again. Instead, he says,

> By the craft of artisans a likeness of your
> living body will be laid out on my bed,
> which I shall embrace, and clasping the hands
> calling your name, my dear wife, I shall seem
> to have you in my arms, though I do not;
> a bitter joy, I suppose, but anyhow
> I may lighten the weight of my soul. And visiting me
> in my dreams you might gladden my heart; for it is sweet
> to see dear ones even at night, even for a while. (ll. 348–56)

This passage has been regarded as extreme and even perverse by some critics. But let us examine what the statue signifies and what the passage means in context. Admetus has promised to stay unmarried and celibate, to abjure any kind of celebration or happiness, and to keep Alcestis' memory always with him. On those conditions she entrusts their children to him. The image he promises to make, like the statue of Hermione, is initially a sign that denotes the woman herself. But because of what he has said and done in the scene during which he uttered his pledge, it has, again as in *The Winter's Tale,* further meaning for him: it is a symbol to him of his loss (the joy it brings is bitter) and of his pledges to her, to her children, and to her memory. The statue is initially seen by Admetus as an attempt to freeze the body and personality of Alcestis in all its aspects, and is intended in this sense to form a link with the dead, as in the case of the statue of Protesilaus.

If the creation of such a fetish seems extreme to the point of absurdity, it is also an indication of Admetus' own character and his reaction to the events which are, after all, of his own making. In her death scene, Alcestis is very clear-headed about what is important to her: that her children be well taken care of by Admetus alone, and that there be no stepmother to take her place. If she is to make the sacrifice, she wants to be properly remembered for it. Admetus thinks on an entirely different plane. While his wife makes practical arrangements for the well-being of her children, he can only think of lost love and his own desolation, which is itself apparently so extreme that one wonders what the point is of accepting her sacrifice. His pledge to make a life-sized doll to take her place in his bed as an answer to her request for fidelity to her memory indicates how little he understands her motives. His sentimental and somewhat muddle-headed reaction is indicative of his character, for he will be equally unthinking in his treatment of Herakles' feelings when he pretends that no one important has died and insists on entertaining the strong-man while a funeral is going on in the house (ll. 509–44). ⟨. . .⟩

On a symbolic level, Herakles initiates a wedding. The Greek wedding consisted in part of the ritual unveiling of the bride (the *anakalypteria*), after which she was escorted to her husband's house. Vase paintings show the bride, veil pulled back from her face, led by the groom, who is accompanied by a *paranymphos* or best man. Here Herakles as *paranymphos* presents the veiled "bride" and unveils her; then Admetus leads her by the hand into the house.

This is also where the statue motif reappears. When Admetus finally takes the veiled Alcestis' hand at Herakles' prompting (ll. 1117–18), he momentarily evokes the image of a work of art apparently well known to his audience—Perseus reaching out to behead the Gorgon Medusa, the monster whose look changed men to stone. "Take courage," says Herakles, "Reach out your hand and take the stranger." "All right, so I do," replies Admetus, "as if I were chopping off the Gorgon's head." Reaching out, he averts his eyes in a pose familiar from sculpture and paintings of Perseus slaying Medusa. Alcestis is motionless, speechless, like a work of art and, at the moment of her return from the dead, a realization of the promised statue.

Therefore, as in *The Winter's Tale*, the resolution is marked by the appearance of a statue which is not a statue and which apparently has the power to turn others to stone as well. However, as in *Suor Angelica*, when the real nature of the statue is revealed, the mistakes of the past and the passing of time seem not to be frozen but rather are undone by Alcestis' return to life. For his compulsive hospitality, Admetus is rewarded not only with his own life but by the return of Alcestis as well. The god has had his way, and the family is reunited. The couple has been symbolically remarried, and life will be better than ever. "Now we'll arrange for ourselves a better life than before!" exclaims Admetus in his last lines. "I won't refuse my good fortune."

Because of Alcestis' statue like appearance in the last scene, she bears the connotation of all the promises that Admetus had made never to accept another woman in his house when he declared he would make her statue. His very acceptance of what he believes to be a different statue-like being appears to violate the meaning of the statue he had pledged to make. The visual reference to a wedding ritual might be a positive sign for the reforming Admetus' marriage at this moment if he had accepted the "bride" knowing she was Alcestis. But instead he receives her before he knows who she is, and this must appear as violation of promise to her: the "statue" he receives is not of Alcestis but, symbolically at least, of the stepmother he promised would never enter his house. ⟨. . .⟩

Subsequently, though he is transformed by joy at his discovery of what has happened, he has learned no lesson from tragic suffering. Alcestis, for her part, contradicts visually his cheerful announcement of a happy ending: she remains as scenery, still carrying the connotation which she had when she entered. ⟨. . .⟩

Herakles departs to his labors, leaving the two alone, with Admetus to "answer his part performed" and Alcestis' deafening silence as his reply.

—Robert C. Ketterer, "Machines for the Suppression of Time: Statues in *Suor Angelica, The Winter's Tale,* and *Alcestis.*" *Drama and the Classical Heritage: Comparative and Critical Essays,* ed. Clifford Davidson, Rand Johnson, and John H. Stroupe (New York: AMS Press, Inc., 1993): pp. 285–86, 287–88.

Plot Summary of
The Bacchae

The qualities of wine are twofold: it can warm the heart and create a sense of peace, or it can make one frenzied and violent. Correspondingly, the mythical worshipers of Dionysus, women called maenads, were prone to both moods. Maenads had no temples in which to worship so they went into the deep, untrodden wilderness, where Dionysus gave them herbs, berries, and wild goat's milk. The women experienced a sense of joy, freedom, and ecstasy in the beauty of nature, yet they also participated in savage, bloody feasts. Agave and her countrywomen represent these mythological worshipers, and the extreme savagery of their practices is highlighted with the tragic spectacle of Pentheus' decapitated head.

The cult of Dionysus, with its mythological grandeur, unpredictability, and ruthless bloodletting, was an apt subject for tragedy, especially since Euripides' plays were performed in honor of Dionysus. Like wine, the play creates a fog of confusion as to who is deluded and who is truly wise. This theme is complicated by Bacchus' vengeful playfulness, Agave's transformation into a savage killer, and Pentheus' transformation from a stubborn, small-minded man into a spellbound megalomaniac. Critic Edith Hall calls the play a "meditation on the very experience of theatre; a mimetic enactment of the journey into and out of illusion, the journey over which Dionysus presides in the mysterious fictive worlds he conjures up in his theatre" (*Euripides* xx).

The play's setting is the façade of the royal palace at Thebes. Smoke rises from the vine-clad tomb of Semele. Dionysus enters. Known as Bacchus, he is the son of Zeus the supreme god and Semele, a Theban princess. His birth was unusual: Zeus' wife Hera was jealous at his affair with Semele, who was pregnant by him with Dionysus. Hera persuaded Semele to request that Zeus appear to her in his divine form, knowing that no mortal could survive such an experience. Zeus, bound by an oath he swore to grant Semele any request, appeared to her as a lightning bolt, but snatched Dionysus out of her womb before she was burned to death. He sewed Dionysus into his thigh.

Disguised as a mortal, Dionysus makes a speech proclaiming his lineage and reveals his plan to secure his status as a god in Greece.

Thebes is the first place he has begun to "rouse to Bacchic cries" (24). He is angry that Semele's sisters have spread a lie that Zeus is not his real father, so he is punishing all the women of Thebes by turning them into maenads, or frantic, possessed revelers who now live on the mountain of Cithaeron. He will continue to punish the city by targeting Pentheus, king of Thebes, who pridefully denies Dionysus' divinity and condemns the bacchanals (revels of Bacchus' followers).

After his exit, the chorus, made of Dionysus' followers, enters singing and dancing the praises of their god. They describe details of the bacchanals, where milk, wine, and honey flow from the soil and the maenads eat raw flesh. Indeed, the bacchic practices are as dangerous as they are joyful.

Teiresias and Cadmus enter, dressed like maenads: each wears a fawnskin and a garland and carries a thyrsus, which is a fennel rod tipped with ivy leaves. Teiresias is a blind prophet and Cadmus is the former king of Thebes and grandfather of Pentheus. These two are the only men of Thebes who have chosen to follow Dionysus, and they believe it is the only reasonable thing to do. The theme "what is wisdom?" begins here, as Teiresias notes ironically that he and Cadmus, aged men who spend their time in dance and frivolity, are the only men who have good sense.

Pentheus enters and condemns the women of his city for spending their time in the "shady mountains" (219) where they "serve the lust of the males" (222-3). He has jailed as many as he can and threatens to decapitate Dionysus if he finds him. When he sees Cadmus and Teiresias he condemns them as well. Teiresias cautions Pentheus to reconsider his position, while Cadmus reminds him that Actaeon was torn to pieces by flesh-eating dogs when he presumed to doubt the power of Artemis, the goddess of the hunt. The chorus interjects their own condemnation of Pentheus' folly. When Pentheus remains stubborn, Teiresias calls him mad and the chorus proceeds to sing of Pentheus' blasphemy and the power of Dionysus' wine to ease sorrow, concluding that "Mere cleverness is not wisdom" (395).

Pentheus' servants bring Dionysus to him, having arrested him. Dionysus is disguised as a mortal and calls himself an initiate of Dionysus. Pentheus questions him condescendingly, while his responses remain flippant, dodgy and playful. Dionysus is taken away to be shut in the stables and Pentheus exits, after which the chorus chants their support of the god, who in turn chants back at them from offstage and causes an earthquake to bring the palace of Pentheus down. The palace is burned, signified by the sudden flaring of fire on Semele's tomb. Dionysus enters and chants to the chorus that Pentheus fought futilely against the gods, first tying up a bull that appeared to him to be Dionysus, then thrusting his sword at a phantom that Dionysus placed in the courtyard. His commentary concludes that "A wise man should always keep a balanced and easy temper" (641), reinforcing a conventional ancient Greek moral that wisdom is in moderation.

Pentheus emerges, shocked that Dionysus is free from the ropes that he thought bound him. A messenger enters and relates a story of the maenads, led by Agave, Pentheus' mother. They were roused out of their peaceful and chaste observance of Bacchic rites by male onlookers who decided to try to seize them. The threat of violence unleashed the violence of the maenads, and at once, the women began to tear cows to pieces with supernatural strength; then they plundered the nearby villages, immune to swords. To the messenger, this proves that a true god is their ruler. The obtuse Pentheus prepares to send his infantry after the weapon-resistant women, but Dionysus convinces him that he can get at the women by first reconnoitering with them, disguised as a reveler. After Pentheus exits, Dionysus makes clear his plan to enact his vengeance on the impious king: he will make a fool of him by dressing him femininely, driving him mad, and leading him to his death. The chorus sings a comment on Dionysus' great plan and asks: "What is wisdom? Or what god-given prize / is nobler in men's eyes / than to hold one's hand in mastery / over the head of one's enemies?" The theme of wisdom begins to incorporate an aspect of revenge and justice.

Dionysus enters, then Pentheus, who is dressed like a bacchant and under his spell. He is delusional and megalomaniacal. After they leave to go to the forest, the chorus sings of Justice's sword dealing the "ungodly, unlawful, unrighteous" Pentheus a mortal blow (1015). A messenger, an attendant of Pentheus, returns to relate what has happened in the forest. Dionysus helped Pentheus perch himself aloft a tall fir so he could see the revelers more clearly, which proved to be a trick, for it made Pentheus highly visible to the women. Led by Agave, they uprooted the tree and fell upon Pentheus, tearing off his limbs, ripping his flesh, and playing ball with it.

Agave, who is carrying Pentheus' severed head atop her thyrsus, enters and is clearly deluded. She believes she is carrying a mountain lion's head, but Cadmus, who has brought the remains of Pentheus on a bier, reorients her to reality by making her look at the sky. She realizes with horror that she is holding her son's head. Because of its element of recall-orientation, this scene has been called the first record of psychotherapy.

Cadmus explains that Pentheus' fate is punishment for his irreverence to the gods and laments that he himself will be banished. Dionysus appears above the house and proclaims that Cadmus and his wife will be changed into serpents and drive an ox-drawn cart at the head of the barbarians. This demonstrates one aspect of divine punishment in Greek mythology; the innocent are punished as well as the guilty when the gods are not reverenced.

Agave will also be banished, and she bids a tearful farewell to Cadmus. The chorus sings a stock ending that is repeated in several of Euripides' plays, which tells of the gods' unpredictability and the many manifestations of divine will. ❀

List of Characters in
The Bacchae

Dionysus is also known as Bacchus. He is the divine son of Zeus and Semele. Angry that Semele's sisters have spread the lie that Zeus is not his real father, he punishes the city of Thebes by turning the women into possessed revelers who kill their king, Pentheus. Dionysus' playacting, disguises, and powers of delusion make him a symbol for the power of the theater itself.

Teiresias is the blind prophet of Apollo. He participates in the bacchanals with Cadmus because he respects the power of Dionysus and knows that he will be punished if he does not reverence this god.

Cadmus is the former king of Thebes, the father of Agave, and grandfather of Pentheus. He, like Teiresias, is alone in believing in Dionysus' immortality. Ironically, this wise old man displays his wisdom by donning the festive garb and reveling in the woods with the women. At the end of the play, it is Cadmus who must explain that Pentheus suffered for his irreverence to the gods, providing the moral lesson before he is banished. Despite his loyalty to Dionysus, he and his wife are sentenced to be transformed into serpents and drive an ox-drawn cart at the head of the barbarians.

Pentheus is the king of Thebes. He does not believe in Dionysus' divinity so is punished by being humiliated and killed. His disgust at the women's revelry in the woods is so violent that many critics have interpreted it as suppressed sexual desire. His *hamartia*, or mistaken judgment, about Dionysus is so severe that he plays right into the hands of his punisher, agreeing to join the revelers in costume and perch himself atop a high tree in full view of them. Before Agave kills Pentheus, he admits he has been wrong and appeals to her as a son to spare him, but she is unable to recognize him and kills him anyway.

The Messenger from the mountain supplies information to the audience about important dramatic action that takes place offstage. He relates to Pentheus that he has seen the maenads in both their peaceful state and their savage, murderous state. The striking contrast between the two moods reflects the dualistic nature of the god they worship.

The Messenger attendant of Pentheus functions to inform the audience of Pentheus' death and the tragic circumstances surrounding it. He tells the chorus of Pentheus' brutal murder by the maenads, in which they ripped off his flesh and played ball with it. This sort of action, not possible on stage, was described by a messenger so that the audience could experience the emotions of pity and fear.

Agave is the daughter of Cadmus and the mother of Pentheus. She is one of the women of Thebes punished by Dionysus. Possessed and in a violent frenzy, she and her womenfolk attack Pentheus when he sits on a treetop to watch them. She decapitates her son and mounts his head on her thyrsus, thinking she has killed a mountain lion, until Cadmus brings her out of her spell. She is horrified at what she has done. The power of Dionysus is clear: he has transformed a loving mother into her son's savage killer.

The Chorus are all Lydian women and devotees of Bacchus. Their sympathies lie with the bacchic worshipers, and they sing in praise of their god and in judgment of the irreverent Pentheus. The chorus also puts forth the question "what is wisdom?" which becomes an important theme in the play. ❀

Critical Views on
The Bacchae

GILBERT MURRAY ON EURIPIDES' ORIGINALITY

[Gilbert Murray (1866–1957) was the regius professor of Greek at Oxford and translator of numerous Greek authors, including Euripides, Aeschylus, Sophocles and Aristophanes. His books include *History of Ancient Greek Literature* (1897), *The Rise of the Greek Epic* (1907), *The Classical Tradition in Poetry* (1927), and *Hellenism and the Modern World* (1953). In this excerpt, Murray shows that Euripides' own originality and freedom emerge paradoxically from the play's old plot and stock characters.]

The *Iphigenia* was all invention, construction, brilliant psychology; it was a play of new plot and new characters. The *Bacchae* takes an old fixed plot, and fixed formal characters: Dionysus, Pentheus, Cadmus, Teiresias, they are characters that hardly need proper names. One might just as well call them—The God, the Young King, the Old King, the Prophet; and as for Agave, our manuscripts do as a rule simply call her 'Woman'. The *Iphigenia* is full of informalities, broken metres, interruptions. Its Chorus hardly matters to the plot and has little to sing. The *Bacchae* is the most formal Greek play known to us; its Chorus is its very soul and its lyric songs are as long as they are magnificent. For the curious thing is that in this extreme of formality and faithfulness to archaic tradition Euripides has found both his greatest originality and his most perfect freedom.

He is re-telling an old story; but he is not merely doing that. In the *Bacchae* almost every reader feels that there is something more than a story. There is a meaning, or there is at least a riddle. And we must try in some degree to understand it. Now, in order to keep our heads cool, it is first necessary to remember clearly two things. The *Bacchae* is not free invention; it is tradition. And it is not free personal expression, it is drama. The poet cannot simply and without a veil state his own views; he can only let his own personality shine through the dim curtain in front of which his puppets act their traditional parts and utter their appropriate sentiments. Thus it is doubly elusive. And therein no doubt lay its charm to the poet. He had a vehicle into which he could pour many of those 'vaguer faiths and aspirations which a man feels haunting him and calling to him, but which he cannot state in plain language or uphold with a full acceptance of responsibility'. But our difficulties are even greater than this. The personal meaning of a drama of this sort is not only elusive; it is almost certain to be inconsistent with itself or at least incomplete. For one only feels its presence strongly when in some way it clashes with the smooth flow of the story.

Let us imagine a great free-minded modern poet—say Swinburne or Morris or Victor Hugo, all of whom did such things—making for some local anniversary a rhymed play in the style of the old Mysteries on some legend of a mediaeval saint. The saint, let us suppose, is very meek and is cruelly persecuted by a wicked emperor, whom he threatens with hell fire; and at the end let us have the emperor in the midst of that fire and the saint in glory saying, 'What did I tell you?' And let us suppose that the play in its course gives splendid opportunities for solemn Latin hymns, such as Swinburne and Hugo delighted in. We should probably have a result something like the *Bacchae.*

For one thing, in such a play one would not be troubled by little flaws and anachronisms and inconsistencies. One would not be shocked to hear St. Thomas speaking about Charlemagne, or to find the Mouth of Hell situated in the same street as the emperor's lodging. Just so we need not be shocked in the *Bacchae* to find that, though the god is supposed to be appearing for the first time in Thebes, his followers appeal to 'immemorial custom' as the chief ground for their worship (201, 331, 370: cf. *Aesch.* fr. 22?), nor to observe that the Chorus habitually makes loud professions of faith under the very nose of the tyrant without his ever attending to them (263 f., 328 f., 775 f.). Nor even that the traditional earthquake which destroys the palace causes a good deal of trouble in the thinking out. It had to be there; it was an integral part of the story in Aeschylus (fr. 58), and in all probability before him. One may suppose that the Greek stage carpenter was capable of some symbolic crash which served its purpose. The language used is carefully indefinite. It suggests that the whole palace is destroyed, but leaves a spectator free, if he so chooses, to suppose that it is only the actual prison of Dionysus, which is 'off-stage' and unseen. In any case the ruins are not allowed to litter the stage and, once over, the earthquake is never noticed or mentioned again.

Again, such a play would involve a bewildering shift of sympathy, just as the *Bacchae* does. At first we should be all for the saint and against the tyrant; the persecuted monks with their hymns of faith and endurance would stir our souls. Then, when the tables were turned and the oppressors were seen writhing in Hell, we should feel that, at their worst, they did not quite deserve that: we should even begin to surmise that perhaps, with all their faults, they were not really as horrible as the saint himself, and reflect inwardly what a barbarous thing, after all, this mediaeval religion was.

This bewildering shift of sympathy is common in Euripides. We have had it before in such plays as the *Medea* and *Hecuba:* oppression generates revenge, and the revenge becomes more horrible than the original oppression. In these plays the poet offers no solution. He gives us only the bitterness of life and the unspoken 'tears that are in things'. The first serious attempt at a solution comes in the *Electra* and *Orestes.*

In a Mystery-play such as we have imagined, re-told by a great modern poet, the interest and meaning would hardly lie in the main plot. They would lie in something which the poet himself contributed. We might, for instance, find that he had poured all his soul into the Latin hymns, or into the spectacle of the saint, alone and unterrified, defying all the threats and all the temptations which the Emperor can bring to bear upon him. There might thus be a glorification of that mystic rejection of the world which lies at the heart of mediaeval monasticism, without the poet for a moment committing himself to a belief in monasticism or an acceptance of the Catholic Church.

—Gilbert Murray, *Euripides and His Age* (London: Oxford University Press, 1965, first published 1918): pp. 92–95.

WILLIAM SALE PSYCHOANALYZES PENTHEUS

[William Sale is the author of *Existentialism and Euripides: Sickness, Tragedy and Divinity in the* Medea, *the* Hippolytus *and the* Bacchae (1977). In this excerpt, Sale examines Pentheus' unconscious restraint of his own sexuality.]

My purpose here is to analyze Pentheus, not to discuss the *Bacchae* as a whole. But the psychoanalytic critic suffers from a questionable reputation, and should welcome the chance to show that his credentials as a man of taste, if not as a scholar, are reasonably well in order. Necessity offers that chance, for a few preliminary remarks on the nature of Dionysus are vital to any analysis of Pentheus, psychoanalytic or otherwise; perhaps while making them I shall be able to give some reassurance as to my own literary sanity. After that I want to go through each of the Pentheus scenes as if it were a session on the couch; then a look at one of the case-histories in the psychoanalytical journals may enable us to reconstruct a life-history of Pentheus' illness. I am not threatening to present a completely unfamiliar play: the reader will have to decide whether I have used the facts of another man's life and another man's illness to illuminate or to strait-jacket the life and illness of Pentheus. But the hard evidence I use will all be taken from the play. If there is disagreement—and I have yet to encounter the psychological interpretation that won much initial favor—it will be over how to interpret what is in the play, not over my dragging in hypotheses from outside that have the approval of famous names in psychiatry. ⟨. . .⟩

We can all agree, I think, that the bull that Pentheus tries to tie up is a symbol for masculinity—*somebody's* masculinity. Does this mean that it stands for aggression, force, power? A bull would certainly work as such a symbol. But it has not been characteristic of Pentheus to try to curb anyone's aggressiveness—it is sexuality and the folly of old men that he hopes to restrain. If ⟨R. P.⟩ Winnington-Ingram ⟨*Euripides and Dionysos* (Cambridge 1935)⟩ is right, and this bull is Pentheus' own animality, then it is his own sexuality; certainly not his aggressiveness, which has been allowed to run rampant from the start. Similarly, when Pentheus slashes away at the phantom Dionysus, I see this as an effort to kill his own libido, to castrate himself psychically. Both here and earlier, he is so vehement, so bull-like, in what he undertakes; he seems to want to say, 'I am a man'. Yet in choosing his sexuality as his target, he seems to want to say, 'I am not a man'. Surely this is why Dionysus tells him that he doesn't know who he is: can you know who you are, if you don't know what sex you belong to?

No good psychoanalyst will allow his symbolic interpretations to go unverified, just as no polite literary critic ought to force them down his audience's throat. Is there any other evidence that Pentheus wants to repudiate his own masculinity? We may note that at the end of the first session we conjectured that Pentheus was deeply afraid of sex within himself. His morbid anxiety over what he imagines women to do when they let themselves go suggests that he is really anxious over what he himself might do, if he were to let himself go. But that was a conjecture, and we shall not use one conjecture to verify another. We shall wait, and if we see Pentheus vigorously asserting his maleness in a healthy way, we shall revise our views.

Pentheus begins what we might somewhat arbitrarily call his fourth session—the prison scene was the third—by listening to a long account of how arms cannot prevail against the Bacchae and immediately issuing a call to arms. Women are powerful: armies must be mustered. Now women *are* powerful—that is an objective fact which our play goes to some lengths to emphasize. But it also emphasizes that physical force is no way to meet that power, and that proposition too, I think, is entirely reasonable. But Pentheus is not reasonable. His infantile fantasies propose savagery, soldiers, swords. In such a spirit he rejects all of Dionysus' pleas. 'Bring me my arms, and *you* stop talking.' Suddenly Dionysus offers the challenge: would you like to *see* them? And against the surge of this temptation Pentheus yields at once—nothing would please him better. All critics of the play agree that Dionysus is now beginning to take over Pentheus' soul. But some seem to regard the god as imposing from outside a madness that has nothing to do with what Pentheus has been all along. This, I submit, is altogether un-Greek and impossible. Dodds himself says that the poet shows us the supernatural . . . working upon and through nature . . . the persecutor is betrayed by what he would persecute—the Dionysiac longing in *himself'*. I would put it a little differently; I would say that the Dionysiac longing is sexual, and that it is bursting forth in the form of *voyeurism*. Dionysus is not to be resisted forever. He will emerge. But Pentheus cannot let him emerge as normal sex. We are watching a phenomenon that has all the signs of *dementia praecox*: the crumbling away of the personality and its defenses through a violent assault of libidinal feeling in the face of a situation, a temptation with which the individual simply cannot cope. The madness, the breakdown, has already begun when Pentheus cried out, bring me my armor! This is an impossible solution, and is immediately relinquished in favor of the voyeuristic wish, which is a compromise. It allows him to join the company of the Bacchae, not as a friendly fellow reveler, but as a hostile spy. At the same time it gives some scope, not dangerous, to his sexuality. Those lewd acts in which the women are engaged—he cannot participate, that would be too threatening. But he can watch it happen, and get his satisfaction vicariously.

But to look, he must first dress as a woman. This he resists at first: *aidos* restrains me (828). A most suggestive remark! Only *aidos* is holding him back; otherwise . . . He wavers—'I cannot'—but the alternative is bloodshed, and his resistance gives way at once. Either fight with women, then, or dress like one. He cannot fight—women are too powerful for that; so he becomes a transvestite, a compromise female. The obvious alternative is not available to him—behave towards them as a grown man behaves towards women, with strength and tenderness.

—William Sale, "The Psychoanalysis of Pentheus in the *Bacchae* of Euripides." *Yale Classical Studies* 22 (1972): pp. 63, 69–71.

WILLIAM C. SCOTT ON THE SYMBOLIC SIGNIFICANCE OF LIGHT AND DARKNESS IN THE PLAY

[William C. Scott is the author of *The Oral Nature of the Homeric Simile* (1974), *Musical Design in Aeschylean Theater* (1984), and *Musical Design in Sophoclean Theater* (1996). In this excerpt, Scott explains that the play's motifs of light and darkness represent the rational and the irrational states of mind.]

Pentheus wants clear and distinct answers to all his questions. He wants to know exactly who this god is, what he does, when and why, and finally what claim this god can make on Thebes. It is significant that during the course of the play Pentheus asks far more questions and gets far more reports than any other character (cf. 460–81; 642–59; and the reports brought to Pentheus—443 ff. and 677 ff). He is continually interested in detailed and definite information.[17] The response to his attempts is discouraging. Dionysus never satisfactorily answers any one of his questions and even tells him that some things cannot be explained to a non-initiate. This is not totally evasion; the stranger is the representative of a mystic religion which is deeply involved with miracle. For a rational man like Pentheus the true answer, "the god did it," is too unclear to satisfy.

This difference in the two characters appears in words and images which are related to clarity and obscurity, namely, light and darkness. Pentheus in his first speech states that the women are racing about on the shady mountainside (218), and in fact, the words "shady" and "dark" are connected with this religion. At 485 he asks the stranger whether he practices his rites during the day or at night; the response is, "Many of them at night; darkness possesses a certain reverence." The grove where the maenads worship is shadowed over by fir trees (1052). The king sarcastically tries to oblige this god by locking him in the darkness of the stables, and the chorus yearns to be like the fawn who seeks shelter in the shady wood (510 and 875). This is also a god of vague and indistinct light—not sunlight or daylight but fire light. In the darkness the Bacchante carries a pine torch (146); the god Dionysus is not constrained by the dark prisons of Pentheus but rather lights a fire at the monument to Semele and casts an illusory blaze around the palace (622 ff.). When he emerges from the dark prison, he is greeted by his worshippers as the "greatest light for us of our Bacchic revelry!" (608 ff.). Dionysus is at home in the darkness or in the ambiguous light which flickers in the darkness.

Pentheus distrusts the darkness because it is dangerous for the women of the town (487); he would prefer to see things done in the open light of day. He feels that it will make the stranger ineffective when he puts him into the darkness (510). Dionysus is suspect because his skin is pale; he has not been in the sunlight but rather seeks the delights of Aphrodite in the shadows (457 ff). Pentheus favors the clear sunlight and dislikes darkness and shadows.

Euripides expresses this motif in several ways. For example, there is no reason for the poet to include Teiresias in this story of Thebes, and yet the seer is deeply involved in the light-darkness theme since he is the blind man who does not see the light of day (210). The blind man, however, can actually see more clearly with his intellect than Pentheus can with his clarity of vision.

Most relevant to this theme is the awakening of Agave at the end of the play:

⟨ll. 1264–67⟩

Previously, while she was in the Bacchic frenzy, her vision was dimmed; when she recovers and can see what she is carrying in her hands, the whole world becomes brighter and clearer.

When Pentheus emerges from the palace under the guidance of Dionysus and says that he can see two suns in the sky, he is losing his precise vision of things as they are. Smokey flames and bright flashes dominate the staging. The sun—the symbol for a clear and distinct view—has now blurred to a double image in Pentheus' view. In this state he goes to his death. He is willing, but only because another of his basic characteristics has been taken from him—his constant insistence on clarity and precision.

Note
[17] Cf. Winnington-Ingram 164 ff. where he lists the words for "seeing" and "understanding;" they are repeated sufficiently to demonstrate Euripides' interest in this theme.

—William C. Scott, "Two Suns over Thebes: Imagery and Stage Effects in the *Bacchae*." *Transactions of the American Philological Association* 105 (1975): pp. 343–45.

CHARLES SEGAL ON THE PLAY'S ENACTMENT OF THE PARADOXICAL NATURE OF TRAGEDY

[Charles Segal's numerous works on ancient literature include *Landscape in Ovid's "Metamorphoses"* (1969), *Tragedy and Civilization: An Interpretation of Sophocles* (1981), *Dionysiac Poetics and Euripides' "Bacchae"* (1982), and *Oedipus Tyrannus: Tragic Heroism and the Limits of Knowledge* (2001). In this excerpt, Segal argues that *Bacchae* enacts the problematic relation between imagination and reality, or illusion and truth, in both art and life.]

In the *Bacchae*, I suggest, Euripides uses the figure of Dionysus as god of the tragic mask to reflect on the paradoxical nature of tragedy itself. Paradoxical, because by creating illusion tragedy seeks to convey truth; by causing us to lose ourselves it gives us a deeper sense of ourselves; and by representing events filled with the most intense pain it gives us pleasure. The paradoxes of Dionysus, therefore, his "liminal" status, his place *between*—between truth and delusion, sanity and madness, divinity and bestiality, civilization and the wild, order and chaos—are in part also the paradoxes of tragedy.

Arguably the play embodies a fin-de-siècle self-consciousness, a reflectiveness on a literary form that was now nearing the end of its creative life. Similar preoccupations seem to occur in Aristophanes' *Frogs*, in which Dionysus is also a major figure, and in Sophocles' *Oedipus at Colonus.* On the other hand, concern with the question of illusion and reality in art is nothing new in Euripides: it is a major issue in the *Helen,* written less than a decade earlier. That such problems concerned Euripides and his contemporaries is also attested by the *Helen* of Gorgias.

Viewed in this perspective, the "problem" of Dionysus in the *Bacchae* is, in part, the problem of the relation between imagination and reality in both art and life. By bringing Dionysus himself on the stage and symbolically enacting the power of Dionysiac illusion, Euripides raises and explores the question of how the "falsehood" of (dramatic) fiction can bring us truth; how, by surrendering ourselves and losing ourselves to the power of imagination, we can in some measure find "ourselves," discover or recover some hidden, unfamiliar part of our identity.

The entire play is both a symbolic and a literal epiphany of Dionysus. Dionysus functions as both a religious and a literary symbol: he is the god of religious ecstasy and the god of the lesser ecstasy of the dramatic performance. Euripides, characteristically, exploits the tension between the religious meaning of the epiphany and its more intellectualized significance as a literary symbol of tragedy. How Dionysus "appears," in what form he reveals himself, both within the framework of the play and within the theater of Dionysus, depends on each spectator's predisposition to the god.

In another sense too, the play is a symbolic enactment and distillation of the two contradictory aspects of Dionysus which the paradox of the *Bacchae* contains. The relationship of reflexivity between the Dionysus who is a character in the play and the Dionysus who is outside the play as the god of the dramatic festival and of the theatrical illusion parallels the tension between the "terrible" Dionysus (*deinotatos*, 861) who brings wild joy or wild madness and the tamed Dionysus who is the patron of the tragic performance.

The play gives the participants in the dramatic spectacle, the audience in the theater of Dionysus, the opportunity to encounter the power of the Dionysiac experience without having to suffer what Pentheus, Agave, and Cadmus suffer. As the scapegoat-king within the play is a surrogate victim for the entire community in its contact with the wild ecstasy of the god, so the play as a whole is a surrogate for the real violence and chaos that the Dionysiac frenzy brings to the ordered structures of civilization. In witnessing the represented rite, the city is spared the potential destructiveness of the actual rite. By sacrificing the mythical representative of order, the poet makes it easier for the city and the citizens to surrender something of their own need for order and to confront their own Dionysiac impulses without the violent and bloody rendings of a literal or an emotional *sparagmos*.

> —Charles Segal, "The *Bacchae* as Metatragedy." *Directions in Euripidean Criticism: A Collection of Essays*, ed. Peter Burian (Durham: Duke University Press, 1985): pp. 156–58.

JOHN E. G. WHITEHORNE ON THE SPECTACLE OF PENTHEUS' REMAINS

[John E. G. Whitehorne is the coauthor of *Strategi and Royal Scribes of Roman Egypt: Chronological List and Index* (1987) and the author of *Cleopatras* (1994) and *Greek Papyri from Kellis* (1995). In this excerpt, Whitehorne discusses the power of the spectacle of Pentheus' fragmented flesh to arouse tragic emotions.]

In recent years the revival of interest in the tragedies as plays for the stage, along with a study of ancient stagecraft itself, has brought about a new appreciation of this aspect of their art. The same years have also seen ancient historians, as well as modern, turning their attention towards what is called 'thanatology', the study of what funerary customs and attitudes towards the dead can reveal about a society's organisation and social structure[2]. In this paper I have tried to draw these two strands of enquiry together to consider briefly just one facet of ancient stagecraft where we see reliance being placed by the dramatist primarily upon spectacle. I call this 'the dead as spectacle', by which I mean not so much the static display of corpses upon the *ekkyklema*, a feature common to many tragedies and one which is often remarked upon, as the use of a body or bodies not only as a momentary point of focus but also as a means of generating further dramatic action. The body's presentation provides the initial visual shock and its impact is then reinforced by other means—the actions and reactions of the actors, the grouping of the chorus and extras, the use of stage properties—as the dramatist works to arouse the tragic emotions. ⟨. . .⟩

In the final messenger speech of the 'Bacchae' (ll. 1043–1152) we hear how, despite Pentheus' pleas for mercy, the Bacchants have torn him limb from limb and scattered his body, engaging in a sort of impromptu game of handball with his mutilated flesh. The speech ends with a reference to the imminent arrival onstage of Agave, still in the grip of the Bacchic frenzy, with Pentheus' head spiked on the point of her thyrsus. The chorus breaks into a little dance of triumph at the death of their persecutor but it quickly runs out of steam as their thoughts turn to horror at what has happened. The beat however picks up again almost immediately as Agave bursts in carrying the head aloft (l. 1168), in the midst of a wild exulting dance[6], a celebration of the hunt culminating in an invitation (l. 1184) to feast on her newly caught prey, the right and proper way to end any successful hunting expedition.

So far we have only heard about the dismemberment of Pentheus even though the messenger's description was cast in exceptionally vivid terms. Now we are to have the spectacle of Pentheus' dead body, or rather its constituent parts, progressively introduced. To begin with, there is the head on the pole thrust high into the air by the jubilant huntress. With its beard and curling locks Pentheus' head calls forth a series of Dionysiac images—a newly cut vine wreath for the halls (l. 1170), a young heifer whose jaw has just started to grow downy under its crest of soft hair (l. 1185), a lion's head for Cadmus to nail up as a trophy on the triglyphs of the palace (l. 1214—with a suitable gesture towards the stage building behind her). We can imagine Agave alternately raising and lowering the head, holding it to her to admire it or thrusting it gleefully into the faces of the chorus whose words show them shrinking back with appropriate gestures of revulsion.

Agave's call to Cadmus to come and admire her prey (l. 1211) is the cue for the old man's entry, followed by bearers carrying the remains of Pentheus. Cadmus is now an exhausted old man, bone-tired from his myriad searchings for the body's scattered pieces in the inscrutable thickets of Mount Cithaeron (ll. 1219–1221), the words he uses as he turns wearily to indicate the bier which the attendants with him have been carrying slowly and carefully down the *parodos*. This is the play's final entrance (not counting the epiphany of Dionysus on the *theologeion*), and like the majority of entrances in the 'Bacchae' it is made stage right, from the country. Yet its slow defeated pace is in deliberate contrast to the bustle (whether of joy, or anger, or agitation, or triumph) of previous entrances made from that direction, the way from which Dionysus had originally come. It is the final sluggish wave of the unstoppable spring tide that breaks over the dyke, and carries all before it.

The remains of Pentheus, covered though they are, have already drawn all eyes. For now we have only the stretcher with its shroud, but it could have been made unpleasantly obvious that it was not a whole corpse which lay beneath the ominous lumps of its covering. Certainly it is evident from Agave's question at line 1300 ('Is everything decently joined up among his limbs?') and from Apsines' summary of this lost portion of the play that the composition of Pentheus' limbs had yet to take place. This, it is clear, was performed on stage by Agave herself and constituted the play's final moment of climax.

Euripides though has yet to exhaust all the dramatic possibilities of his first stage property. Agave still holds Pentheus' severed head. At some point during the course of Cadmus' entry she has transferred it from the tip of the thyrsus into her arms (l. 1238) and is cuddling it almost like a child. The movement of laying down the thyrsus and grasping the head to her, ready to proffer it ceremonially to her father, represents visually the double role Agave currently occupies, as both housewife and huntress (both stressed in the preceding lines) and foreshadows the difficult transition which still awaits her from one back to the other. She now holds it out to Cadmus to hang up on the housefront, repeating as she does so her invitation to feast on the animal's flesh.

That flesh is now no longer imagined, as it had been when the chorus shrank from the same invitation earlier. It is actually there physically onstage before us under the covered bier, every moment of whose long slow entry we have just been watching. Although the corpse itself is not yet visible, we see its effect in Cadmus' abrupt reaction for as well as the pity and revulsion shown earlier by the chorus there is now a new element of violence in his rejection of Agave's invitation. Agave's reply speaks of how bad tempered and scowling he has become with old age (ll. 1251–1252).

The head is next put to another use in what has been called the play's 'psychotherapy scene'[7]. So far it has been used as a plaything, as a hunting trophy, and as an object of dread to both the chorus and Cadmus. Now it is to be used therapeutically as Cadmus brings his daughter slowly back from hysteria. He begins by concentrating her gaze on external matters (ll. 1264 ff.), and then has her recall her own personal history (ll. 1273 ff.) and so regain her identity as an individual before getting her to focus upon the head itself (line 1277) and finally explore its meaning for her.

There can be no doubt that this is a climactic moment, when Agave realises for the first time that this is no lion's head she has in her arms but the head of her own son. Yet it was not the play's final climax, with the *deus ex machina* brought hurriedly on to tie up the loose ends, leaving the sight of Pentheus' head as the last image of horror as the 'Bacchae' winds down to its conclusion.

Notes

[2] The appearance within the same year of review articles in both J. R. St. and J. H. St. (J. A. NORTH, J. R. St. 73 (1983) 169–174; S. R. F. PRICE, J. H. St. 103 (1983) 195–197) and of a popular anthology, 'The Oxford Book of Death' (Oxford 1983), demonstrates the growing interest in the subject at all levels.

[6] The parallelism between Pentheus' exit, dancing, at line 970 (as W. STEIDLE, Studien zum Antiken Drama (Munich 1966) 37, suggested) and Agave's entry, dancing, here, is deliberate. From that point on the god is totally in control.

[7] See G. DEVEREUX, J. H. St. 90 (1970) 35–48.

—John E. G. Whitehorne, "The Dead as Spectacle in Euripides' 'Bacchae' and 'Supplices.'" *Hermes* 114 (1986): pp. 59–60, 60–62.

MARY R. LEFKOWITZ ON EURIPIDES' TRADIONALISM IN PORTRAYING THE POWER OF THE GODS

[Mary R. Lefkowitz is the author of *The Lives of the Greek Poets* (1981), *Women in Greek Myth* (1986), and *Not Out of Africa: How Afrocentrism Became an Excuse to Teach Myth as History* (1996) and the coeditor of *Black Athena revisited* (1996). In this excerpt, Lefkowitz uses the *Bacchae* to refute the notion that Euripides' treatment of the gods is impious.]

Of the three dramatists, it is Euripides who makes his audience most keenly aware of the gods' interest in human affairs. Nine of his nineteen surviving plays conclude with scenes where gods speak from the stage machine;[2] in four plays gods speak the prologue;[3] Iris and Lyssa appear, dramatically—and with terrifying effectiveness—in the middle of the *Heracles*. Only six plays have no gods as characters, though in four of these the audience hears about or sees a miraculous event that could only have been brought about by a god: Medea appears with the bodies of her children in the chariot of Helios; in the *Heraclidae* we learn how in the midst of the battle against Eurystheus (Heracles' persecutor) Heracles and his bride Hebe, the goddess of youthful vigour, appear as a pair of stars near the chariot of old Iolaus, Heracles' nephew, and make him young again, just for the day of the battle (851–8); as Agamemnon prepares to sacrifice his daughter Iphigenia, the goddess Artemis makes the girl disappear and puts a deer in her place (*IA* 1580–95). In the *Hecuba* the murderer of Hecuba's son Polymestor is told by Dionysus that Hecuba, who has blinded him and murdered his children, will be turned into a dog whose tomb will be a landmark for sailors (1265–74). Only in two plays, the satyr play *Cyclops* and the *Phoenissae,* does no miracle occur.

Yet despite the frequency with which Euripides portrays in his dramas the gods and their actions, he is thought of as the poet who more than any other asks his audiences, ancient and modern, to question the nature of the gods and even their existence.[4] The notion that the poet himself had doubts about traditional religion, even to the point of being atheistic, derives from his own dramas, or rather from Aristophanes' and other comic poets' versions of them.[5] In the *Thesmophoriazusae,* a woman claims that Euripides has spoiled her livelihood (selling wreaths for statues of the gods) because 'by working in tragedies he has persuaded men that the gods do not exist' (450–1). The comic Euripides in the *Frogs* prays to 'other, private gods': 'Ether, my food; Pivot of my tongue, Comprehension, and Nostrils keen to scent' (888–93). In the *Thesmophoriazusae* he tells a story of creation in which Ether, rather than Earth, is the mother of all living things (14–15). In the *Frogs*, according to his adversary Aeschylus, he is 'an enemy of the gods' (836). ⟨. . .⟩

But although Euripides' 'philosophizing' made him seem impious, at least to the comic poets and the biographers who used their works as 'evidence', I believe that it can be shown that any character in Euripides who expresses 'philosophical' notions about the gods does so out of desperation, and that ultimately, the gods in that play will prove—not always to the characters' satisfaction—that the gods still retain their traditional powers. Perhaps understandably, modern scholars often seem uncomfortable with such an austere notion of divinity. But let us review the passages where characters in plays criticize the gods or question their motives or even their existence,[9] considering the nature of the gods' behaviour in the dramas where characters complain of them, and comparing (wherever possible) Euripides' portrayal of the gods with those of Homer and the other dramatists. ⟨. . .⟩

Can Euripides in the *Bacchae* be recommending the pious acceptance of irrationalism? Walter Burkert has characterized these lines as an expression of the paradox that the state that produced Socrates condemned him and other rationalists to death: 'Pentheus, the sensible defender of rational order, is drawn to a wretched end; irrationalism rises against enlightenment.'[21] But to speak of Pentheus as a 'sensible defender of rational order' does not correspond with the facts of the play, where Pentheus' conduct is neither sensible nor rational; as the messenger states from his more objective standpoint: 'I fear your quick judgments, master, your sharp temper and your too imperious bearing' (670–1). The issue, as Euripides describes it, is not irrationalism vs. enlightenment, but whether or not it is desirable to have the cult of the god Dionysus in Thebes. From the beginning Euripides makes it clear that the dances and rituals of the god will bring at best a mixed blessing to the city. Participants in his rites are required to act contrary to the conventional rules of behaviour: they must wear a strange get-up that strikes Pentheus as absurd and foolish (250–2), and the rites of Dionysus are celebrated mainly at night, a time that Pentheus, like most Greek men, considers 'treacherous and corrupt for women' (487). Nonetheless, the consequences of rejecting the cult are even worse: the god drives the women mad, so that they abandon their homes and live in the mountains and behave like wild beasts. To portray such undesirable alternatives does not amount to condemnation of the gods; as Achilles says in the grim context of the last book of the *Iliad*, from his two jars of good and evil Zeus offers man a mixture, or all evil (524–33).[22] As a dramatist, Euripides' purpose is to describe ancient myth in realistic and vivid terms; and his lesson, if anything, as in other Greek religious ritual, is to do honour to the gods and, in the process, to remind men of their mortal limitations.[23]

Notes

[2] Gods *ex machina* in *Hipp., Suppl., El., Ion, IT, Hel., Or., Ba., Rhes.*, cf. Antiope: cf. W. S. Barrett, *Euripides, Hippolytus* (Oxford, 1964), p. 395; O. Taplin, *The Stagecraft of Aeschylus* (Oxford, 1977), pp. 444–5. Possibly also *Phaethon, Rhadamanthys* (PSI 1286 = Hypothesis 14 Austin), *Erechtheus, Phrixus, Archelaus* (cf. test 7, A. Harder, *Euripides Kresphontes and Archelaos* [Leiden, 1985], p. 174).

[3] Gods speak in the prologues of *Alc., Hipp., Tro. Ba.*

[4] E.g., most recently, C. P. Segal, *Dionysiac Poetics and Euripides' Bacchae* (Princeton, 1982), pp. 335–6, 'the monumentalizing effect of these lines [*Ba.* 1325–6] again puts the truth about divinity in the form of an absence'; cf. H. Foley, *Ritual Irony: Poetry and Sacrifice in Euripides* (Ithaca, 1985), p. 258, 'Euripides can find no order outside ritual and myth and rational speech, yet in the end the order provided by art, ritual, and speech remains in an uncertain relation to the reality of the contemporary world'; cf. S. Goldhill, *Reading Greek Tragedy* (Cambridge, 1986), p. 234; A. Michelini, *Euripides and the Tragic Tradition* (Madison, 1987), pp. 315–20. On the development (from Romanticism) of this modern attitude, see esp. R. Schlesier, 'Goetterdaemmerung bei Euripides?', in *Der Untergung von Religionen*, ed. H. Zinser (Berlin, 1986), pp. 35–50; H. Lloyd-Jones, *The Justice of Zeus* (Berkeley, 1983), pp. 151–5; Michelini, p. 108.

[5] For details, see my 'Was Euripides an Atheist?', *SIFC* [Ser. III] 5 (1987), 149–66.

[9] Not including the notorious fragment of the *Sisyphus* (Critias, fr. 1 N) sometimes attributed to Eur., cf. M. Winiarczyk, 'Nochmals das Satyrspiel "Sisyphos"', *WS* 100 (1987), 35–45.

[21] W. Burkert, *Greek Religion*, tr. J. Raffan (Cambridge, MA, 1985), p. 317.

[22] Cf. Eur. fr. 661 N from the beginning of the *Sthenseboea*.

[23] Cf. Dodds (n. 11), pp. xlv–xlvi.

—Mary R. Lefkowitz, "'Impiety' and 'Atheism' in Euripides' Dramas." *The Classical Quarterly* 39, no. 1 (1989): pp. 70–71, 72, 75.

VALDIS LEINIEKS ON PENTHEUS' ERRONEOUS PERCEPTION

[Valdis Leinieks is the author of *Morphosyntax of the Homeric Greek Verb* (1964), *Index Nepotianus* (1976) and *The Plays of Sophokles* (1982). In this excerpt, Leinieks shows that Pentheus' faulty perceptions are never corrected; thus he dies ignorant.]

The relationship between observation and correct and erroneous perception is explored in the earthquake scene. The scene contains three events which are universally observable. The three events are described twice, once by the chorus and once in the report of the Stranger. The first event is an earth tremor (585) caused by Dionysos, which shakes the house of Pentheus. Part of the chorus call to the rest to observe (591) that the stone beams are gaping apart (592). The Stranger later explains that at the time Dionysos came and shook the house (623). The next event is a fire on the tomb of Semele caused by a lightning bolt sent by Dionysos (594, 596–599). The chorus again inquire of each other whether they observe (596) the fire. The Stranger later comments that Dionysos lit the fire (623–624). The third event is a second earth tremor, again caused by Dionysos, which causes the house to collapse (600–603). The Stranger later comments that Dionysos has thrown the house to the ground (633). None of these events is observable as such by the audience, but they are convincingly conveyed to them by the words and dance movements of the chorus. The three events are observed and perceived both by the chorus and by Dionysos and can be thought of as universally observable and the same for everybody.

Pentheus' perception of these events is entirely different. He fails to perceive the first earth tremor. At the time (622) he is occupied in trying to tie up the Stranger whom he has imprisoned in the stable. He perceives that he is tying up the Stranger (616). As a universally observable and perceivable event, however, his action consists of tying up a bull that he has found in the stable (618–621). The Stranger sits by and quietly observes (622) and perceives the event correctly. The reason why Pentheus has formed an erroneous perception of the event is that he is feeding on his expectations (617). Pentheus perceives what he expects to perceive, not what can be derived from the universally observable. His expectation-based perception, in turn, is derived from an already established perception. He perceives that he has imprisoned the Stranger in the stable, expects to perceive him there, and does perceive him there. Pentheus is also not one who hesitates to act on the basis of his perceptions. In this instance he applies himself to the absurd task of tying up the bull with the utmost intensity. He bites his lip and drips sweat from his body (620–621). In addition, he displays much anger (620). Intense activity and strong emotion are characteristic of the state of frenzy. Pentheus next forms an erroneous perception about the fire on Semele's tomb. He observes (624) the fire on the tomb, but since he does not expect a miraculous fire on the tomb, he forms the erroneous perception that the palace is on fire (624). Once more he exerts himself to the utmost on the basis of his perception. He runs back and forth giving orders to his servants (625–626). Since the house is not on fire, they all toil in vain (626). Pentheus also fails to perceive the second earth tremor. This time he is occupied in trying to kill the Stranger. Dionysos lights a torch (630; 631)[21] in the courtyard, which Pentheus mistakenly perceives as the Stranger. According to his perception the Stranger has escaped into the courtyard and he expects to perceive him there. Pentheus rushes inside with his sword drawn (628) and stabs at the flame (631) perceiving that he is killing the Stranger (631). Dionysos then shakes the palace to the ground (633), an event which Pentheus does not perceive. ⟨...⟩

The most serious consequence of Pentheus' inability to perceive anything that contradicts already established perceptions is that it makes it impossible for him to correct erroneous perceptions. He is not able to learn. Once he has formed a perception, whatever its source, he is not able to change it. His perceptions of Dionysiac rites, Dionysos, and the Stranger, although not originally his own, remain unchanged in spite of overwhelming evidence to the contrary. He is unable to perceive the power of Dionysos in spite of repeated demonstrations, because for him Dionysos does not exist. The only experience that he is able to learn from is the extraordinary experience of his imminent death. He perceives that he is about to be killed (1113) and begs Agave not to kill him (1118–21). For the first time ever he is able to perceive that an established perception of his is wrong. In the process he confesses to errors (1120–21). His confession of errors, however, does not mean that he has necessarily learned anything far-reaching and insightful.[22] He has perceived the

power of Dionysos and learned that Dionysos is a god. This much
had been predicted by Dionysos himself (859–860). There is no indication that Pentheus has suddenly learned that he should avoid the
use of force and follow customary practices. Pentheus' words here
can be contrasted with Kreon's in the *Antigone*. Kreon has learned
that it is best to follow customary practices (1113). Pentheus
remains as ignorant in death as he had been in life about the proper
way men should live.

Notes

[21] For a discussion of the text, see chapter XVII.

[22] Winnington-Ingram (note 1). "He understood his physical danger; of greater
insight there was, and could be, nothing, nor should we read too much into his
ultimate admission of error." (165–166)

—Valdis Leinieks, *The City of Dionysus: A Study of Euripides' Bakchai*
(Stuttgart: B. G. Teubner, 1996): pp. 239–40, 241–42.

DANIEL MARK EPSTEIN ON RELIGIOUS ECSTACIES IN ANCIENT AND MODERN TIMES

[Daniel Mark Epstein is the author of several books of
poetry, including *The Boy in the Well* (1995) and *The Book
of Fortune* (1982). He has written for the *Atlantic,* the *New
Yorker,* and the *New Republic* as well as for the off-
Broadway stage, and he translated Plautus' comic play
Trinnumus from the Latin. In this excerpt of the preface to
his translation of *The Bacchae*, Epstein compares Dionysian
religious fervor in Euripides' time to present-day charismatic Christianity.]

The Bacchae shows us the conflict between Pentheus, Prince of
Thebes, and the new God, Dionysus. Pentheus returns from a
journey to find that his city has been turned upside down by this
strange God of wine, who leads packs of women to revel in the hills
of Cithaeron, where they indulge in ecstatic "orgies." Pentheus
declares war on the Bacchantes, denying their God and his priest,
who we soon discover is Dionysus in disguise.

Pentheus is the guardian of the State. He is the protector of law and order: these depend on reason, and on good citizens living safely within their senses. Dionysus is the irrational energy that inspires humankind, the animal instinct that makes humans one with Nature. Dionysus is the force that drives men and women to ecstatic heights, in drinking, dancing, hunting, war, and sex—and always in praising the God. Properly understood, all these pleasures are forms of devotion, ways of prayer.

The theme of *The Bacchae*, the struggle between cold reason and emotional ecstasy, is universal and simple when applied to the individual. But the way history reflects the conflict—in revolutions, persecutions, and religious revivals—is extremely complex and difficult to convey. It is easy enough for an armchair philosopher to talk of "eternal verities" and tell us that human nature does not change. But the playwright and the translator do not deal in generalities, they deal in hard facts, concrete details and specific situations.

One does not render a milieu in generalities but in the poetry of things. It may please the structural anthropologist to say we are like the ancient Greeks in our essential human desires, fears, and spiritual concerns. But is it really true? At the end of the fifth century B.C., generations of war and militarization had led to such a strict ordering of public life in some Greek city-states that many people felt stifled by the rule of reason. They yearned for a greater indulgence in beauty and pleasure, a more intimate connection with nature. The reaction in Delos was the cult of Dionysus. Mobs of men and women drank themselves out of their senses, went running on the hills hunting wild animals, tearing them apart, and eating them alive, before settling down to more wine-drinking, dancing, and sexual free-for-alls in the forest.

All this, mind you, was done in a fervent atmosphere of religious devotion to the God. And this was not the eccentric behavior of a few outlaws but a broad-based religious revival tolerated if not sanctioned by the state.

Are we like those ancient Greeks who sanctioned the cult of Dionysus? No. The strict social conformity and political witchhunts of the Eisenhower era gave way to the ecstasies and excesses of the 1960s. Yet we did not hunt in packs and eat wild animals alive on mountain paths, nor were our ecstasies religious, for the most part.

There were many pseudo-religions and many false gods during the Vietnam War, but these were not sanctioned by the majority.

If Americans want release from what Blake called the "mind-forged manacles," most of us do not seek it in Nature. These days, a more serious challenge to rationalism—in numbers and respectability—is the revival of fundamentalism in America. At the end of this century, the fastest-growing segment of Christianity is the "charismatic" movement, which values the emotional, ecstatic experience of union with Christ above the cooler rationalism of denominational Protestantism. But these charismatic Christians do not glory in the flesh. Unlike the ancient Greeks, most Americans deny the human body and the natural world as sources of mystical redemption; they distrust any ecstasy outside the walls of a church.

So the translator's main challenge is to render the ancient Greek conflict in contemporary terms. This is a humbling task. We are flawed mirrors of history. The Victorian translator whose choruses echoed the Presbyterian hymnal was doing his best to render the Bacchants' piety in contemporary language; so was the scholar of the 1950s who made his women choristers drawl with accents of existential irony. Now both of these scripts seem dated, counterfeit, quaint. We want, on the one hand, a certain purity of diction, a timeless flow of images and rhythms that the years will not betray. On the other hand we want the freshness of a voice rooted in the present, in the real world—in short, *in history.* Hence the paradox: the best translation must sooner or later become dated. The more concerned the play is with manners and customs, the sooner that translation is likely to spoil. Renderings of *Medea,* largely concerned with the personality and psyche of the protagonist, will last longer than *The Bacchae,* which relates a social upheaval in arcane religious terms.

I wished, in 1968, that Peter Brook would stage a version of *The Bacchae* with sex, drugs, and rock and roll, reflecting the decade's conflict between reason and passion, order and ecstasy. It did not happen. And now I think that if it had such a version would not have survived the deaths of Janis Joplin and Jimi Hendrix.

—Daniel Mark Epstein, "Translator's Preface." *Euripides, 1: Medea, Hecuba, Andromache, The Bacchae,* ed. David R. Slavitt and Palmer Bovie (Philadelphia: University of Pennsylvania Press, 1998): pp. 219–21.

Plot Summary of
Medea

A truly complicated character, Medea displays brilliant, machiavellian savagery, mourns her state as a woman scorned by her husband and the conventions of her civilization, and underscores her cold, calculating plan of revenge with a passionate desire for a husband she lost. Also complex is the relationship between gods and mortals: Medea's airborne escape at the end of the play shows the gods to be advocates and facilitators of Medea's vengeful extremism. Philip Vellacott points out that Euripides' attitude toward the gods is distinct in that he presents them as "amoral cosmic or social forces, blind and often destructive in their operation; powers which man can apprehend if not explain, but which are themselves incapable of understanding the spiritual qualities of man or the values by which he lives" (Introduction to *Euripides: Three Plays* 9–10). Just as the gods seem amoral, Medea lives by her own rules, leading critics to debate whether Medea is in fact a champion of women or a tragic self-saboteur.

All of the action in this play takes place outside Medea's house in Corinth. The Nurse comes out of the house and makes a speech lamenting Medea's losses and imminent destruction. She refers to the story of Jason and the Argonauts. The story the nurse does not detail follows thus: with her knowledge of magic and her intense love for him, Princess Medea of Colchis helped Jason obtain the golden fleece in her own land for King Pelias, who had usurped the kingdom of Iolkos from Jason's father. To avenge Pelias' treatment of Jason and his father, Medea convinced his own daughters to kill him, after which she and Jason were forced to flee to Corinth because the people of Iolkos were horrified at what she had done. Medea and Jason had a marriage ceremony and two children, but eventually Jason betrayed Medea and their children and married Glauce (Creusa), the daughter of Creon, king of Corinth, thus securing his own safety and eventual kingship. Now Medea hates her children because they remind her of Jason's betrayal, and the Nurse is afraid Medea's fiery and vengeful temperament will lead her to harm them.

The Tutor enters with Medea's two children and reveals to the Nurse that Creon plans to banish Medea and her children from

Corinth. The Nurse is appalled at Jason's lack of concern for his children, but the Tutor in his cynicism chides her for forgetting that "everyone loves himself more than his neighbour, some justifiably, others simply to improve their situation . . ." (lines 86–87). The Nurse tells the Tutor to keep the children away from their mother, comparing Medea's rageful eye to that of a bull. At this point the theme of Medea's animalism is introduced.

Offstage, Medea chants her woes, wishing ruin to Jason and her children and death to herself, and admitting to being the killer of her own brother. She refers to cutting her brother up in pieces and throwing them into the ocean so that her father Aeetes would be preoccupied and delay his pursuit of her. Meanwhile the Nurse and the Chorus chant to each other in grief and concern.

Medea enters from the house and proclaims her wretchedness. She laments the plight of women, who are forced to lay down a fortune to get a husband and find themselves trapped and alone in the home if the marriage goes badly. Meanwhile, men can escape the home if they do not like the responsibility of marriage and find company elsewhere. She proclaims "I would rather stand three times in the battle line than bear one child" (lines 251–52), and warns that "In all other respects a woman is full of fear and proves a coward at the sight of iron in the fight, but when she is wronged in her marriage bed, no creature has a mind more murderous" (lines 264–67). There is an enormous intensity given in this play to the anger of a woman sexually wronged, which initially provokes the audience's pity and fear.

Creon enters, telling Medea that he will exile her because he fears she will take revenge. Medea convinces him to let her stay one more day so she can plan for her children, playing on Creon's sympathy and his love for his own children. When Creon leaves, Medea coldheartedly declares her plan to murder Jason, his wife, and Creon.

Jason enters, smugly criticizing Medea for her immoderate behavior and for bringing this punishment on herself. Medea responds by castigating him for abandoning her after all she sacrificed for him, and Jason retorts that women's moods are ruled by the quality of their sex life and they are more trouble than they are worth. His smugness and self-important attitude about his sexual betrayal of Medea builds sympathy for Medea while casting him as evil. The chorus sings of the virtues of moderation and temperance in love, equating Jason's violent passion with lack of virtue and ultimate ruin, and they proclaim their sympathy for an unpitied Medea.

Aegeus, king of Athens, enters. He is on his way back from Apollo's oracle at Delphi where he received guidance on his state of childlessness. Medea convinces him to give her refuge in his home, promising him in return to give him medicine for his problem. At Medea's request, he makes a solemn pledge to help her, swearing by the Earth and the Sun. The Sun is actually Medea's grandfather, father to Aeetes, Medea's father.

After Aegeus leaves, Medea reveals her plan to the Chorus. She will convince Jason to keep the children and send them bearing gifts to Glauce to win her affections. But the gifts will be poisoned and kill her. Then she will kill her children to make Jason miserable. She will prove to all that she is not "weak and submissive, a cipher" but "dangerous to my enemies and good to my friends" (lines 808–10). Though the chorus protests, Medea is determined.

Jason enters in response to Medea's request to see him. She admits to being foolish and rageful and claims to have come to reason. She convinces him to persuade his new wife to accept the children and ask Creon to let them stay. She sends Jason away with the children, who will innocently present a poisonous robe and headband to Glauce to obtain her favor. When Medea's children return having delivered the gifts, she feels guilt and agonizes over whether or not to kill the children. Here her complexity becomes stunning; she can be murderous as well as hold tender feelings for her children. She convinces herself to follow through with her plan.

A messenger enters to tell the grisly story of Glauce's fate. Despite her initial scorn for the children, Glauce could not resist the adornments that they brought and put them on before a mirror in delight. Then the robe and headband slowly ate through her flesh, causing her an agonizing death. Her grieving father suffered the same fate as he leaned over her and became inescapably stuck to her poisonous garments. The messenger concludes that "no man is ever truly happy. One may have better luck than another if wealth pours in— but that is not real happiness" (lines 1228–30). While Medea goes in the house and kills the children, the Chorus sings to the Earth and Sun of Medea's wretchedness and ill fate.

A grieving Jason enters, intent on saving his children from Medea's fury, but the Chorus tells him he is too late. Medea appears above the palace. She is with her dead children in a chariot drawn by dragons. She mocks Jason for trying to get into the house and swears he will never lay a hand on her. She gloats that Zeus, the Sun and her grandfather have provided her with her chariot to get away. In his anger and shock, Jason shouts insults at Medea; he renews his original affront to her by saying "you killed them because our sex life was over" (1339) and calls her an "artist in obscenity" and a "polluted murderess" (1347–48). Medea retorts that he can call her what he wants, but "I have done what I had to—I have stung your heart" (1360–61).

Medea rejects Jason's request for the bodies of his children. She will bury them safely at the precinct of Hera to prevent enemies from raiding their tombs. Medea predicts Jason will die a humiliating death by being hit with a fragment of his ship. The legend bears out her prophecy: Jason's death comes when he is struck in the head by a plank that falls from the Argo.

Jason, moved as never before by love for his children, asks Medea if he may touch them, but she refuses, telling him that he already rejected them. In his grief Jason wishes he had never begot them. Medea flies away in her chariot and the chorus sings a concluding message, which is that "the gods bring many things to pass against our expectation" (1417). ❀

List of Characters in
Medea

The Nurse of Medea opens the play with a background story of the events that have led Medea to her present predicament: she has lost her husband for another woman, and now her "hatred has corroded everything" (17). The nurse's sympathy for Medea, which comes in her harsh judgment of Jason's betrayal, is overridden by her concern for the children, as she tells the children's tutor to keep them away from their dangerously angry mother. Her concern proves to be prophetic.

The Tutor to Medea's children brings the message to the Nurse that Medea will be exiled by Creon, thus informing the audience of Medea's imminent danger and building sympathy and fear for her plight. When the tutor tells Medea that Jason's new bride has accepted his children, he provides the tragic irony. He tells Medea "One of these days your children will bring you home" (1015), when in fact Medea will bring them home, dead.

Medea's two children are victims in her plot to avenge her husband Jason. She kills them in order to make him feel the intensity of pain she has felt at his betrayal. Because they are children who innocently love their mother even up to their death, their power to create pity in the audience is formidable.

Medea is the former princess of Colchis. She fell in love with Jason and helped him obtain the golden fleece from her own land with her magic, and they fled to Corinth with their two children. Because she now feels betrayed by Jason's marriage to Glauce, the daughter of Creon, she plots to kill him and Glauce, then also kills Creon and her own children. Medea's main complaint is having been sexually wronged by Jason, which she argues is a serious enough crime to merit the vengeance she wreaks. At the end of the play, as she escapes with the bodies of her children in a dragon-drawn chariot, she remains bitter at Jason and gloats that she has succeeded in wounding his heart.

Creon is the king of Corinth and father of Glauce, Jason's new wife. He falls victim easily to Medea's manipulation, as he comes to her initially to exile her from the kingdom and agrees at her pleading to let her stay one more day. In effect, he aids her in her murderous plot by letting her stay. He dies as he embraces his dead daughter's poisonous garments, which eat away his flesh just as they did his daughter's.

Jason is Medea's former lover and husband. Though Medea has helped him obtain the golden fleece and bore two children for him, his passion for her has died and he treats her smugly and with contempt. He accuses her and all women of being chiefly motivated by sex, saying that Medea would not be so angry if he had not taken another woman. Jason and Medea bring out the ugliness in each other, and they bicker viciously. Jason's only tender moment comes when he sees his two dead children in Medea's chariot and grieves that she will not let him touch them. Medea's revenge devastates him, while increasing the bitterness he feels for her.

Aegeus is the king of Athens and another pawn in Medea's plot of revenge. When he visits Corinth, on his way from consulting Apollo's oracle at Delphi about his state of childlessness, Medea plays on his sympathy for her as a parent, convincing him that she has been abandoned and persuading him to give her refuge in his home when she escapes Corinth. In return, she promises to give him medicine for his problem. This exchange highlights Medea's razor-sharp cunning and opportunism.

The Messenger returns from Creon's palace to tell the story of Glauce's and Creon's grisly deaths, as their flesh was eaten away slowly by the poisonous garments Medea sent as a gift. The messenger fulfills his conventional purpose, which is to apprise the audience of dramatic action that happens offstage, and to create intense emotions in connection with that action.

The Chorus are made up of Corinthian women, and they initially sympathize with Medea because they judge Jason to be cruel and insensitive. Their loyalty to Medea turns to caution and forbidding judgment when they find out how she is planning to avenge Jason's betrayal. In a curiously cynical moment, they chant that those who have no children are the happiest because they spare themselves of "ceaseless torment" and anxiousness (line 1100). ❀

Critical Views on
Medea

GILBERT MURRAY ON EURIPIDES' REALISM

[Gilbert Murray (1866–1957) was the regius professor of Greek at Oxford and translator of numerous Greek authors, including Euripides, Aeschylus, Sophocles, and Aristophanes. His books include *History of Ancient Greek Literature* (1897), *The Rise of the Greek Epic* (1907), *The Classical Tradition in Poetry* (1927), and *Hellenism and the Modern World* (1953). In this excerpt from the introduction to his translation of the play, Murray argues that Euripides' treatment of the ugliness of revenge is historically accurate but poetically unsatisfying.]

For concentrated dramatic quality and sheer intensity of passion few plays ever written can vie with the *Medea*. Yet it obtained only a third prize at its first production; and, in spite of its immense fame, there are not many scholars who would put it among their favourite tragedies. The comparative failure of the first production was perhaps due chiefly to the extreme originality of the play. The Athenians in 432 B.C. had not yet learnt to understand or tolerate such work as this, though it is likely enough that they fortified their unfavourable opinion by the sort of criticisms which we still find attributed to Aristotle and Dicæarchus.

At the present time it is certainly not the newness of the subject: I do not think it is Aegeus, nor yet the dragon chariot, much less Medea's involuntary burst of tears in the second scene with Jason, that really produces the feeling of dissatisfaction with which many people must rise from this great play. It is rather the general scheme on which the drama is built. It is a scheme which occurs again and again in Euripides, a study of oppression and revenge. Such a subject in the hands of a more ordinary writer would probably take the form of a triumph of oppressed virtue. But Euripides gives us nothing so sympathetic, nothing so cheap and unreal. If oppression usually made people virtuous, the problems of the world would be very different from what they are. Euripides seems at times to hate the revenge of the oppressed almost as much as the original cruelty of the oppressor; or, to put the same fact in a different light, he seems deliberately to dwell upon the twofold evil of cruelty, that it not only causes pain to the victim, but actually by means of the pain makes him a worse man, so that when his turn of triumph comes, it is no longer a triumph of justice or a thing to make men rejoice. This is a grim lesson; taught often enough by history, though seldom by the fables of the poets.

Seventeen years later than the *Medea* Euripides expressed this sentiment in a more positive way in the *Trojan Women,* where a depth of wrong borne without revenge becomes, or seems for the moment to become, a thing beautiful and glorious. But more plays are constructed like the *Medea.* The *Hecuba* begins with a noble and injured Queen, and ends with her hideous vengeance on her enemy and his innocent sons. In the *Orestes* all our hearts go out to the suffering and deserted prince, till we find at last that we have committed ourselves to the blood-thirst of a madman. In the *Electra,* the workers of the vengeance themselves repent.

The dramatic effect of this kind of tragedy is curious. No one can call it undramatic or tame. Yet it is painfully unsatisfying. At the close of the *Medea* I actually find myself longing for a *deus ex machinâ,* for some being like Artemis in the *Hippolytus* or the good Dioscuri of the *Electra,* to speak a word of explanation or forgiveness, or at least leave some sound of music in our ears to drown that dreadful and insistent clamour of hate. The truth is that in this play Medea herself is the *dea ex machinâ.* The woman whom Jason and Creon intended simply to crush has been transformed by her injuries from an individual human being into a sort of living Curse. She is inspired with superhuman force. Her wrongs and her hate fill all the sky. And the judgment pronounced on Jason comes not from any disinterested or peacemaking God, but from his own victim transfigured into a devil.

From any such judgment there is an instant appeal to sane human sympathy. Jason has suffered more than enough. But that also is the way of the world. And the last word upon these tragic things is most often something not to be expressed by the sentences of even the wisest articulate judge, but only by the unspoken *lacrimae rerum.*

—Gilbert Murray, *The Medea of Euripides* (New York: Oxford University Press, 1912): pp. ix–xi.

PHILIP VELLACOTT ON MEDEA AS CHAMPION OF
OPRESSED WOMEN

[Philip Vellacott has translated the plays of Aeschylus,
Euripides, Menander, and Theophrastus and is the author
of *Sophocles and Oedipus: A Study of* Oedipus Tyrannus,
with a New Translation (1971) and *The Logic of Tragedy:
Morals and Integrity in Aeschylus' Oresteia* (1984). In this
excerpt, Vellacott highlights the subversiveness of Medea's
speech on the unfortunate status of women in marriage.]

The Nurse's opening monologue provides a balanced portrait.
Medea has behaved well in Corinth, but she had contrived murder in
Iolcus. She is a 'frightening woman'; but she is also the mother of
two little boys; and now the two men on whom her life depends,
Jason and Creon, are planning together to get rid of her. Her passionate devotion to Jason had been acceptable while it made her an
obedient wife (13–15); when it makes her resent infidelity her husband sees it as a barbarous excess. But though this balanced portrait
is important to the drama, there is equal or greater significance in
the symbolic function of Medea as an heroic figure championing the
whole female world.

She can champion womankind because she is in no sense an
average woman. Like her predecessor Clytemnestra, she is the
female representative of those miraculous Athenian generations
whose men dethroned tyranny, established law and a sovereign
people, defeated the Persian Empire, organized the Delian League,
sent ships and soldiers adventuring all over the eastern Mediter-
ranean, created the theatre, invented history, founded science,
refashioned architecture, design, oratory, argued with Anaxagoras
and Socrates—and who in this vast range of achievement gave neither share nor scope to women, apparently never reflecting that the
potential energy for these expanded activities must be present to a
comparable degree in the other sex. Medea is a foreigner; this provides the Athenian audience an acceptable explanation of her
crime of infanticide, leaving her emancipated intelligence and
indignant words free to have their full impact in a statement of
women's wrongs. It has been more than once pointed out that all
through the play Medea's role as champion of oppressed woman is
closely connected with her motherhood (this too links her with

Clytemnestra). This is central to what Euripides has to say here about the injustice which fifth-century Hellas inflicted on women. Not only were they excluded from all but the smallest share of the exhilarating freedoms won by men, but they, and they alone, could bring up a new generation of men, to forget their debt to their mothers and keep wives and sisters and daughters in subjection. Jason is interested in his sons in so far as they are necessary to the establishment of his honourable position as head of an *oikos*, a 'house'; yet, in the prospect of begetting new children from Glauce, he has accepted Creon's sentence of banishment for his sons as well as for Medea; and his mild consent (941) to Medea's request that he ask Creon to let the boys stay in Corinth, does nothing to suggest that his indignation in the final scene arose from any real love for his sons. Creon loves his children, he says (329), even more than his country, and so is open to Medea's plea that she needs one day's grace to arrange for her own children's welfare. Aegeus feels his whole life threatened because he cannot beget children. This essential part of a city's life is the function of woman, as necessary and as exacting as that of the hoplite behind his shield (251); this function has love as its beginning, and can be carried out only by the exercise of love. But if a father's love is like Jason's, what is a mother to do? And what would happen to a city if its women, discouraged by men's abuse and waste of love, were to reach the conclusion voiced by the chorus in 1081–1115, that the sorrows of motherhood outweigh its joys, and choose to be childless? ⟨. . .⟩

From the Homeric age down to our own century there have been rare periods and scattered places where it was possible for a woman to have some say in the choice of the 'possessor of her body'; for the overwhelming majority of women who have ever lived, this has been a freedom often longed for, always denied. Human dignity has been preserved, heroism achieved, ordinary life lived and endured, within this condition of bodily enslavement; and the rare protests against this condition—of which Medea's must be among the most direct to survive from the ancient world—have been heard as Canute was heard when he ordered the tide back. Medea details the additional difficulties experienced by a foreign wife in a Greek city; but after two lines she is again talking about the position common to all Greek wives—a position where, if you are unlucky in your husband, 'death is better' (238–51):

Still more, a foreign woman, coming among new laws,
New customs, needs the skill of magic, to find out
What her home could not teach her, how to treat the man
Whose bed she shares. And if in this exacting toil
We are successful, and our husband does not struggle
Under the marriage yoke, our life is enviable.
Otherwise, death is better. If a man grows tired
Of the company at home, he can go out, and find
A cure for tediousness. We wives are forced to look
To one man only. And they tell us, we at home
Live free from danger, they go out to battle—fools!
I'd rather stand three times in the front line than bear
One child.

After this the poet allows those who wish to forget what she has said to forget it, for she adds (252),

But the same arguments do not apply to you and me—

when in fact everything she has said, except for 238–9, applies as much to every Greek wife as to a foreigner.

Let us look closely at this manifesto. First Medea points out the absurdity that in marriage it is the slave who is forced to buy herself a master; bodily slavery (233) is bad enough, without having to pay money for it. And a woman is not even allowed to choose a man who seems likely to be a good husband; if she is given a bad one, divorce can be got only at the cost of ill repute; if she does not seek divorce, he may rape her every night of her life. Thus to preserve sanity and dignity demands in some marriages the skill of a magician. A man can find other women when he tires of his wife; a woman has no such escape. Finally, an answer to what Orestes says to Clytemnestra in *Choephori* 921, 'it is the man's work that feeds the woman who sits at home.' Medea points out that, though a man by working or fighting preserves the city, the city itself, and the citizen, exist only because a woman bore a son. Every item in this survey of woman's position applies to contemporary Athens; it may be a pessimistic statement, but in fact no girl contemplating marriage could be sure that her lot would not answer exactly to this description. The statement, moreover, has a peculiar, and significant, dramatic untruth. Medea, speaking in anger, forgets that she herself, being a woman in ten thousand, had in fact chosen her own mate; her only dowry was the help she gave Jason in stealing the Golden Fleece. Her manifesto, then, is spoken less on her own behalf than on behalf of all the women of Athens. Further, though what she says is factually untrue about herself, it truly indicates the character and attitude of Jason. And because it is a stark presentation of current facts to men who are reluctant to consider them, this is the one place in the play where such a direct statement can have a properly dramatic function, before the events of the drama have yet begun to move. Subsequent emotions will safely erase from the audience's memory this subversive challenge.

—Philip Vellacott, *Ironic Drama: A Study of Euripides' Method and Meaning* (Cambridge: Cambridge University Press, 1975): pp. 106–7, 107–9.

BERNARD KNOX ON MEDEA'S SUPERHUMAN QUALITIES

[Bernard Knox's many works include *Oedipus at Thebes* (1957), *Essays Ancient and Modern* (1989), and *Backing into the Future: The Classical Tradition and Its Renewal* (1994). In this excerpt, Knox examines the ways in which Medea exhibits characteristics of a god, while refuting the argument that the play champions women's rights.]

Medea is presented to us not only as a hero, but also, at the end of the play, by her language, action and situation, as a *theos* or at least something more than human. She does not start that way, but that is how she ends. Ends, that is to say, in *this* play:[52] she is going to Athens, as she tells us, and what form she will assume there we are not told. It is not likely that Euripides' audience was worried about that point: they must have been sufficiently taken aback by the appearance of Medea, the murderer of her sons, in the 'habiliments of the goddess', assuming the attitude and using the language of the stage *theos*.

It is very hard to imagine what it meant to them (and what it should mean to us), for there is no parallel to it in Attic drama. Peleus in the *Andromache* is told that he will become a *theos* (1256) and given a rendezvous for his apotheosis (1265ff.), but it does not take place on stage. Helen, at the end of the play which bears her name (1667), is given a similar assurance (not fulfilled on stage) and in the *Orestes* she actually appears on the right hand of Apollo, on her way to rejoin Castor and Polydeuces in the heavens (1631ff.), but she does not say anything. There *are* two cases in which a human being at the end of the play performs one of the functions of the *deus ex machina*. Eurystheus, in the *Heraclidae*, on the point of death gives instructions for his burial (1036) and reveals a Delphic oracle which gives his buried corpse protective powers for Athens in future wars (1032ff.). (However he expressly forbids a cult of his grave 1040–1.) In the *Hecuba*, the blinded Polymestor prophesies the transformation of Hecuba, the deaths of Agamemnon and Cassandra (1259ff.). These are faint and partial approximations but there is nothing remotely comparable to Medea's full exercise of all the functions of the *theos* and her triumphant god-like departure through the air.

The effect of this investment of Medea with all the properties and functions of stage divinity must have been to bring home to the audience the conviction that Medea is not merely an individual woman wronged and revengeful; she is, at the end, a figure which personifies something permanent and powerful in the human situation, as Aphrodite clearly does, and Dionysos also. These two were Olympian deities, worshipped in state cult and portrayed in temple-sculpture, but the Greek imagination created many other *theoi*, was apt, in fact, to see a *theos* in every corner. 'All things are full of gods' said Thales, and from Hesiod on through the fifth and fourth centuries, Greek literature presents us with *theoi* who represent almost every phase of human activity and circumstance—Poverty, Plague, Reputation, Force, Helplessness, Ambition, Time and Sorrow, to name just a few. A sentence of Menander gives a clue to what lies behind this proliferating theogony: adding a new *theos* to the unofficial pantheon—Shamelessness (*Anaideia*)—he says: 'Whatever has power is now worshipped as a god.'

Medea, in her last appearance, certainly has power but it is not easy to define exactly what she represents. There is a *theos* in Aeschylus which bears some resemblance to her: the house-destroying *theos* of the *Seven against Thebes* (720–1). But this *theos* is almost immediately (723) identified as an *Erinys*, and that will not do for Medea; in fact, as a spiller of kindred blood she should be their allotted victim, as Jason vainly hopes she will be (1389). Revenge—*dike* in the simplest sense—certainly has something to do with it, but she is more than Lesky's 'Dämon der Rache';[55] there would have been no need to give her the style and appurtenances of a *theos* for that—as seems clear from the figure of Hecuba in the last scenes of the play which bears her name. Perhaps the appearance of this ferocious incarnation of vengeance in the place of an Olympian god is meant to reinforce in the audience's mind that disconcerting sense of the disintegration of all normal values which the play as a whole produces, to emphasize visually that moral chaos which the chorus sang of earlier:

> The spell cast by sworn oaths has faded; respect for others no longer remains anywhere in Greece, it has taken wing up to the sky (439ff.).

But Medea as *theos* must also represent some kind of irresistible power, something deeply rooted in the human situation, as dangerous as it is universal. It has something to do with revenge for betrayal but its peculiar ferocity must stem from the fact that before she was a hero and through her action became a (stage) *theos,* she was a woman.

It is clear from Medea's very first speech that this strange drama, which uses Sophoclean heroic formulae to produce a most un-Sophoclean result, is grounded in the social reality and problems of its own time. There can be no doubt, to anyone who reads it without prejudice, that the *Medea* is very much concerned with the problem of woman's place in human society. I do not of course mean to revive the idea, fashionable in the early years of this century, that Euripides is a 'feminist'.[56] Even though tradition has it that speeches from the *Medea* (in the translation of Gilbert Murray) were read aloud at suffragette meetings (a careful selection, no doubt), it is not likely that Sylvia Pankhurst would have admitted Medea to membership in the League. Euripides is concerned in this play, not with progress or reform,[57] but (just as in the *Hippolytus* and the *Bacchae*) with the eruption in tragic violence of forces in human nature which have been repressed and scorned, which in their long-delayed breakout exact a monstrous revenge. The *Medea* is not about woman's rights; it is about woman's wrongs, those done to her and by her.

Notes

⁵² Cf. Cunningham, 'Medea', p. 159: 'Although this final appearance of Medea involves an illusion that she is a *theos*, we are also reminded that it is not a true apotheosis . . . She is going off to Athens to live with Aegeus there.'

⁵⁵ *Tragische Dichtung³*, p. 309.

⁵⁶ L. Bloch, 'Alkestisstudien', *Neue Jahrbücher*, Band 7 (1901), 30: 'In seinem Herzen, stand er auf der Seite des damals gerade in mächtiger Bewegung aufwärtsstrebenden Geschlechtes.' Bloch refers with approval to Ivo Bruns' 'feine und richtige Beobachtung' (in *Frauenemancipation in Athen* (Kiel 1900), p. 9) 'dass Euripides die an Zahl noch geringe fortschrittliche Partei der athenischen Frauen in den Chorliedern der "Medeia" zu Worte kommen lässt.'

⁵⁷ Cf. K. J. Reckford, 'Medea's First Exit', *TAPA* xcix (1968), 239: 'This is not to say that Euripides is acting as the women's champion . . . or writing social criticism or pleading for some reform.'

—Bernard Knox, "The Medea of Euripides." *Yale Classical Studies* 25 (1977): pp. 208–11.

HELENE P. FOLEY ON MEDEA'S PASSION AND REASON

[Helene P. Foley is the author of *Ritual Irony: Poetry and Sacrifice in Euripides* (1985), *The Homeric Hymn to Demeter: Translation, Commentary, and Interpretive Essays* (1994) and *Female Acts in Greek Tragedy* (2001). In this excerpt, Foley asserts that Medea's passion and reason operate in harmony.]

Those who read the monologue as a struggle between reason and passion view Medea's story as a tragedy of sexual jealousy. In the famous closing lines of her monologue (1078–80), the irrational passion for revenge (*thumos*) provoked by Jason's sexual betrayal is seen in their view to be at war with her rational *bouleumata;* passion wins. In my view, this is the Roman dramatist Seneca's Medea, not Euripides'. Seneca's Medea does allow her passion to subdue her reason. Euripides' Medea, whenever she explains her decisions, is proud of her intelligence and unashamed of the complex emotional and rational motives that she has for her actions; throughout the planning of her revenge, passion and reason explicitly operate in concert.¹¹ Medea is quite capable of recognizing that emotion can lead her to make critical errors. At 485 (see also 800–801) she complains that she was more eager (*prothumos*) than wise when she allowed her love for Jason to lead her to commit crimes against her family and to depart from her homeland. She also knows that decisions can be arrived at through a suppression of passion by reason (although she uses no technical terms to this effect), but she never makes this a goal in her own decision making. This is partly because the control or devaluation of emotions by rational deliberation is an ethical mode that she associates with the despised Jason. Thus at 598–99 Medea rejects Jason's practical rationalization for the marriage with the princess on the grounds that she wants no happiness won with pain. Jason claims to Medea that he has not been motivated by desire in his decision to marry the princess (556); he has considered (*bebouleumai*, 567) his actions and their consequences and so can claim to be *sophos* (548) in the plans he has made. In her second interview with Jason, Medea pretends to apologize for her anger (*orgas*, 870; see also 883) and lack of good sense (882, 885). She has engaged in discussion with herself (*logon*, 872; *bebouleumai*, 893) and decided to give up her anger (*thumou*, 879). Having considered her children's welfare and her impending friendless exile, she says she has come to a better understanding. Jason, pronouncing Medea's anger understandable, is delighted that after reflection Medea has accepted the superior plan (his own: *boulēn*, 913). But this is all playacting on Medea's part; she cleverly mimics Jason's own mode of ethical reasoning and feigns female subservience only in order to deceive her adversary. Although she is in full control of her reason throughout,[12] Medea never elsewhere indulges in such bloodless decision making; indeed, she aims in her revenge precisely to make Jason feel the emotions he once rejected (1360, 1370).

As would be expected in a debate that pits a maternal Medea against an avenging Medea (rather than reason against passion), there are rational as well as emotional or counter-rational considerations on both sides of Medea's internal conflict concerning the children. On the one hand, Medea first rationally reflects that killing the children will bring punishment to herself as well as to Jason and will destroy her own future (1021–39); the sight of the children with their breathtaking childish beauty and innocence then reawakens vivid maternal feelings (1040–43). Yet to the Medea who advocates revenge these maternal arguments instantly appear "soft" (1052 at 677 such soft words are associated by Medea with female subservience and deceptiveness); insofar as they violate from this opposing perspective her self-interest and reputation, the arguments of the mother are in Medea's view counter-rational. On the other hand, we come to Medea's monologue with an accumulated knowledge of all her motives for revenge, both rational and irrational, although in the speeches in which she addresses her revenge plans she stresses the rational motives for her act.[13] We have, of course, been told repeatedly from the beginning of the play that Medea is enraged at Jason's erotic betrayal of her, and in the closing scene she eloquently defends being motivated in her revenge by *erōs:* "Do you think bed [*lechos*], then, a trivial pain for a woman?" (1368; see also 265–66, 1354). Justice is an even more important motive (see 26, 160, 165, 578, 580, 582, 592, 1352–53). Medea has sacrificed her homeland for Jason; she has incurred many enemies in order to help her husband (483–87, 506–8). Jason has made his plans without thinking of the welfare of either Medea or the children. He has thus in Medea's view wronged his friends, while she has kept her side of the bargain by giving him heirs (470, 696, 698; 490–91). Above all, Jason broke his oath to Medea, an oath sworn by the gods (20–23, 161, 439, 492, 1392);[14] Medea is for this reason quite certain that the gods will support her punishment of Jason. And the final surprising appearance of the chariot of the sun seems to prove her right.

Notes

[11] In this respect I disagree with Fortenbaugh, who makes the most extensive proto-Aristotelian reading of the passage. Fortenbaugh argues that Medea often engages in Aristotelian practical ethical reasoning, in means–ends deliberation. But with Medea it is not, as in Aristotelian practical reasoning, a simple case of emotion proposes, reason disposes. She is motivated from the start in her revenge plans by justice and intellect as well (see below for further discussion). Medea does not reason against emotion in wanting to spare the children, or reason about emotion (Fortenbaugh 238n) in the monologue. As Dihle 28–29 points out, one cannot distinguish in Medea Aristotle's two forms of ethical reasoning, practical planning and the moral control of reason through emotion.

[12] See *manthanō* in 1078. Despite the Nurse's fears of Medea's heroic, almost bestial wrath, the Medea we see on stage never seems close to *mania* or irrationality.

[13] See Bongie 42 and 44, on Medea's first scene with Jason, and Dihle 14–16.

[14] On the importance of Jason's breaking of the oath, see esp. Burnett and Flory.

—Helene P. Foley, "Medea's Divided Self." *Classical Antiquity* 8, no. 1 (1989): pp. 63–65.

BERND SEIDENSTICKER ON MEDEA'S MASCULINE ROLE

[Bernd Seidensticker is the author of *Die Gesprachsvedrichtung in den Tragödien Senecas* (Heidelberg, 1969) and *Palintonos Harmonia: Studien zu komischen Elementen in der griechischen Tragödie* (Gottingen, 1982), as well as of numerous articles and reviews on Greek and Roman drama. In this excerpt, Seidensticker shows that Medea's loss of happiness as a wife and mother causes her to adopt a masculine role.]

Although Medea is certainly more the sister of the masculine Clytemnestra than of the feminine Deianira, one can nevertheless find a number of parallels to the latter as well. For Medea (as for Deianira) her husband is the center of her life. For her love of Jason she has sacrificed everything; for Jason she has betrayed her father, left her native land, and during her flight, in order to save her lover, killed her own brother. Expelled from Iolcus, she now lives in Corinth, a stranger, isolated, except for her husband and children. At the very moment when she finally hopes to find peace, her husband, whose life she saved more than once, decides to leave her and to marry the daughter of Creon, the king of Corinth. Her life is destroyed (225–229). The situation is aggravated by the fact that the king fears her revenge and wishes to expel her from the city and that she does not know where to find a new shelter for herself and the children (502–505). Totally isolated and deeply hurt in her sense of loyalty and justice as a wife, in her pride as a woman, and in her love of Jason, she decides to take revenge.

> For in other ways a woman
> Is full of fear, defenseless, dreads the sight of cold steel;
> But, when once she is wronged in the matter of love,
> No other soul can hold so many thoughts of blood.
> (263-266)

Here too it is not the case that Medea resists marriage and confinement to the *oikos* or "that she has subordinated her feminine skills to a purely masculine desire to dominate," as Shaw puts it. Rather, as in the cases of Clytemnestra and Deianira, we have a violation of the female sphere by the husband, and here too the reaction takes place in the woman's own domain and with the typically female weapons: cunning, fabric, poison. She invokes Hecate—the goddess of magic and witchcraft who resides in the hearth, the very center of the house (395ff.)—to help her and kills Creusa, her rival, and her father, the

82

king, who, as *kyrios,* is responsible for the marriage, by means of a poisoned gown that she sends to the bride as a wedding gift. Yet this is not enough; in order to completely destroy her treacherous lover and unfaithful husband, she uses, after poison and fabric, the most horrible of possible female weapons, the murder of her own children.

For one who, in a terrible perversion of her sacred duties as daughter, sister, wife, and mother, has destroyed her family, first in Colchis and now in Corinth, no return to any form of a family context is possible. In the end Medea disappears out of the spectator's sight in a serpent-chariot. The destruction of her happiness as a wife and mother forces her, like Clytemnestra, into a masculine role. And the price she has to pay for her revenge is high. Not death, like Clytemnestra, but the loss of herself as a woman and mother.

Other Euripidean women appear to be cast in a similar mold. Creusa, raped by a god and forced to expose her newborn child, finally reacts with cunning and poison when her last hope of finding her son has been disappointed and her husband, with the help of her divine lover, appears to introduce an extramarital son into the family and onto the throne. Electra hates Clytemnestra and Aegisthus not—like her Aeschylean and Sophoclean sisters—because these two have killed her father, but because, by marrying her off to a poor farmer who has not touched her, they have deprived her of a suitable marriage and of children. She helps Orestes kill their mother with a sword, but her main contribution to the matricide is cunning, and she uses a particularly female trick when she lures Clytemnestra into the deadly trap by sending her the message that she has borne her first grandchild. Hecuba endures sheer endless suffering; in the end, however, when she must face the fact that a supposed friend of the royal house has killed her last son, she takes a revolting revenge on the murderer, and she takes it inside, with female cunning and female weapons. She entices Polymestor into her tent, where she and her servants first kill his sons with daggers they have hidden in their robes, and then blind him by piercing his eyes with brooches. But Hecuba also has to pay the price for the brutal revenge with the loss of humanity; as her victim predicts, she will be changed into a bitch.

—Bernd Seidensticker, "Women on the Tragic Stage." *History, Tragedy, Theory: Dialogues on Athenian Drama,* ed. Barbara Goff (Austin: University of Texas Press, 1995): pp. 162–64.

ELEANOR WILNER ON THE PLAY'S CYNICISM

[Eleanor Wilner is the author of four books of poetry, including *Otherwise* (1993), and her writing has appeared in numerous anthologies and periodicals. In this excerpt from the preface to her translation of *Medea*, with Inés Azar, Wilner asserts that the play seriously questions the concepts of piety and human dignity, and its main character Medea is a nihilist and an egocentric.]

⟨. . .⟩ I realize now that back then both this reader, and the critics and scholars of Classical literature whose readings provided the prevailing lenses through which the work was seen, had one thing in common: piety. And piety, which was the built-in attitude toward all the Classical authors and other monuments on which Western culture founded its sense of original genius and continuous identity, was precisely—I now think—the most misleading lens through which to view a drama whose central target is piety, along with heroism, belief in moral order, and high or happy expectations of any kind whatsoever. Translating the play was to open a kind of Pandora's box without the butterfly of hope, and to raise anew the question of what it is that lasts.

The Chorus, Jason, Creon, and Medea all mouth pieties their actions or their next speech belie. The difference between Medea and the other characters in this regard is that she is aware of her (and their) duplicity, and uses that awareness to manipulate the others. She knows well the weaknesses their vaunted or pious words conceal—and plays on the particular vanities of each character. She is a Machiavel without a country to rule—her cause is her own injured pride and power, and the tragedy of Medea, if tragedy is indeed the right word for this brand of truth, is not only that her scale is outsize for the scope of her role in life, but that the logic of the perfect revenge of the cornered person has a Samson-like side—her revenge is surgically exquisite, her enemies are destroyed, and, in a manner of speaking, she has pulled down the house on her own head.

Her house had, of course, been her cage, even as her sense of humiliation was sharpened by her circumstantial dependence on a hollow man into whom her passionate nature and thwarted power once poured full force, a husband for whom she has obvious and, we can surmise, longstanding contempt. From such a power imbalance—she having the innate, he the institutionalized power—comes the time-honored saying "Hell hath no fury like a woman scorned." To understand that, it is necessary to hear simultaneously under that last phrase another—"like a woman's scorn." It surfaces in Medea's clear statement of the purpose of all this blood: "But what is grief compared to the ridicule of fools?"

The nihilist chill of those words reaches the bone when we recall the spilled blood from which that grief arises. The dead children are both fact and metaphor, for on what future, what innocence or principle or hero can the audience now rely? At the end of the *Medea* the future seems empty, almost unimaginable—and it is perhaps that, as much as its psychological acuity, which makes the play seem so unfortunately appropriate to our own moment. There is, as well, the equally appropriate fact that her connections with the past have twice been savagely cut by Medea's own hand, and this for the sake of her passion. In this she may be the Western original for that person who has become all too familiar to us today—the radically disconnected self pursuing personal desires in an egocentric universe.

—Eleanor Wilner, "Translator's Preface." *Euripides, I: Medea, Hecuba, Andromache, The Bacchae,* ed. David R. Slavitt and Palmer Bovie (Philadelphia: University of Pennsylvania Press, 1998): pp. 3–5.

EDITH HALL ON THE PLAY'S RECEPTION

[Edith Hall is the author of *Inventing the Barbarian: Greek Self-Definition Through Tragedy* (1989), has translated Aeschylus' *Persians* (1996), and is coeditor of *Medea in Performance 1500–2000* (2000). In this excerpt, Hall examines the character of Medea in light of the expectations of Euripides' original audience.]

Medea may have failed to please because it ends with the barbarian murderess flying off to take up the offer of a safe haven in Athens that she had earlier extorted from Aegeus. Nor may the audience have enjoyed watching one of their kings expatiate on the subject of his infertility: the Athenian tragedians tend to take care to portray mythical Athenians with dignity. Moreover, the international situation in 431 meant that Athens was in no mood to see any refugee from Corinth, even in myth, demanding favours or asylum.

The play must have been ethically shocking. Medea stands alone amongst tragic felons in committing her offence with impunity. In extant Greek tragedy no other kin-killers reach the end of their plays unpunished. Euripides slightly ameliorates this scandal by suggesting that Medea, as granddaughter of the Sun, is not quite mortal and thus not entirely accountable to ordinary theological rules. Indeed, we never fully understand whether she is mortal or divine, a wronged and sympathetic wife or an agent of divine justice, for Euripides has confusingly also given her and Jason some of the most 'human' dialogue in ancient Greek. The play at one level is but 'a bourgeois quarrel between an obtusely selfish man and an over-passionate woman'.[7] The vengeful, competitive, and sexually honest Medea, in escaping unpunished, was any Athenian husband's worst nightmare realized.

Medea had been previously implicated in murder on the Euripidean stage, in his *Peliades* of 455 BCE. But the shocking effect of the actual infanticide was exacerbated because Euripides almost certainly invented it. His Medea is also the first known child-killing mother in Greek myth to perform the deed in cold blood; the others (Ino, Agave, Procne) seem always to have been given the 'excuse' of temporary madness. This permits Euripides to introduce the extraordinary soliloquy where Medea has difficulty steeling herself to the slaughter (1019–80). But it also leaves the most disturbing crime in extant Greek tragedy premeditated, its culpability undiminished even by mental disturbance.[8] Alone amongst the plays in this volume Medea exemplifies the distinctively Euripidean use of children. There is no evidence for children in Aeschylus, and Sophoclean children (e.g. Antigone and Ismene at the end of *Oedipus the King*) seem to have been non-speaking characters. But Euripides fully exploits the opportunities for pathos the children present: we see them long before Medea, and their death cries represent one of the most heart-breaking moments in Western theatre.

The emotional motor of Euripides' *Medea* renders it one of the more apparently 'timeless' of ancient tragedies: the despair, humiliation, and vindictiveness of a woman abandoned by her man in favour of a younger model speak loud across the centuries. Yet there are features specific to Athens in the second half of the fifth century, in particular the question of Medea's acceptability as an alien to her new city state. At Athens the possession of citizenship was tied to the descent group, and guarded with paranoid anxiety. In 451/450 BCE the statesman Pericles had initiated a law excluding from citizen privileges all but those who could prove that both their parents were members of Athenian citizen families. In 431 BCE Jason's plight may have elicited understanding if not actual sympathy from its male audience: Medea stresses that a barbarian wife could cause embarrassment (591–2). One way of looking at Jason is as a man trying to make a life in a xenophobic new city, while burdened with a wife who was not only not local but not even Greek. From an Athenian perspective Medea's ethnicity must have cast doubts even on the legitimacy of the union's unfortunate offspring.[9] Medea's difference from the women of Corinth must have been emphasized, moreover, by her clothing and appearance: Euripides was almost certainly the first poet to turn her from a Corinthian into a barbarian.

But the unenthusiastic original reception of this play cannot be wholly dissociated from Medea's betrayal of 'femininity'. She fundamentally repudiates the gender role assigned to her as a woman in fifth-century Greece. From her very first monologue (which also marks her first exit from the 'feminine' sphere of the house), and its extraordinary focus on the 'masculine' notions of 'cleverness' and citizenship, we know this is no ordinary woman. She combines in one psyche the 'feminine' qualities of compassion and maternal love with the 'masculine' heroic values of honour, status, and revenge.[10] Yet by the end of the play the inadequacy of the existing sociolinguistic distinctions between public and private, friend and foe, and especially between woman and man, has been unmasked through the characters' failure to communicate except in the most dislocated of linguistic modes. If Euripides' characters did indeed speak 'like human beings', then human beings undergoing marital breakdown have not changed much, after all.

Notes

[7] D. W. Lucas (trans.), *The Medea of Euripides* (London, 1949), 3.

[8] On the child-killing, see P. E. Easterling, 'The Infanticide in Euripides' *Medea*', *YCS* 25 (1977), 177–91.

[9] See further Edith Hall, *Inventing the Barbarian* (Oxford, 1989), 172–81.

[10] Helene Foley, 'Medea's Divided Self', *CA* 8 (1989), 61–85.

—Edith Hall, "Introduction." *Euripides: Medea, Hippolytus, Electra, Helen,* trans. James Morwood (Oxford: Oxford University Press, 1997): pp. xv–xvii.

Plot Summary of
Iphigeneia at Aulis

The tragic force of *Iphigeneia at Aulis* comes from the agonizing changes of heart and mind that the main characters undergo. Agamemnon vacillates between murderousness and tenderness toward his daughter, a warm Clytemnestra stiffens and becomes cold to her husband's folly, and Iphigeneia changes from happy fiancée to indignant victim and finally to deluded, ecstatic martyr. All action of the play is set in front of Agamemnon's tent at Aulis, a place situated on the coast of the strait of Euripus, which separates the island of Euboea from Boeotia in mainland Greece. Euripus, with its ruthlessly changing currents, functions as an analogue to the dramatic action, in which the characters' unpredictable shifts in resolve are meant to create the requisite turbulence in the audience's emotions.

The first 48 lines of the play are lyrical and meant to be chanted. In these, Agamemnon, king of Argos and commander of the Greek army, paces outside his tent in a fit of insomnia brought on by a guilty conscience. His servant, the Old Man, observes him writing and erasing on a wax tablet and asks him what is troubling him. Agamemnon then gives a speech explaining that of Leda's three children, Clytemnestra became his wife and Helen became the wife of Menelaus, Agamemnon's brother and king of Sparta. But Paris fell in love with Helen and took her away while Menelaus was gone. Because all the suitors to Helen have made a solemn pact to Tyndareus, husband of Leda and former king of Sparta, that they would oust any man who dared take Helen away from her eventual husband, the Greek army is now set to make war on Troy to gain Helen back.

Yet, the winds of Euripus are uncharacteristically silent and the Greek army could not sail. So Calchas the seer announced that in order to secure divine help, the Greeks must make the sacrifice of Agamemnon's daughter Iphigeneia to the goddess Artemis. The Greek army persuaded Agamemnon to follow the prophet's orders and so Agamemnon conveyed a message to his wife Clytemnestra to send Iphigeneia to Aulis on the pretence that she will marry Achilles. Now Agamemnon is racked by guilt and has decided to send a countermand to repair his dishonor. He orders the Old Man to deliver his message, composed on his writing tablets, with great speed.

A chorus of women from Chalcis in Euboea enters. They are young married women, aptly suited to observe the dramatic action with attentiveness and emotional intensity. In general, the purpose of the classical chorus is to supply information about events occurring offstage, provide comment on the action in a way that encourages the audience to experience pity and fear, and offer moral or philosophical commentary on the events taking place. This chorus' excited, descriptive portrayal of what they have just seen—the Greek armada poised for battle—gives the audience a panoramic view of what cannot be seen onstage. They sing due praise to the great men at the helms of their ships, including Achilles, son of Thetis who was raised by Chiron, a civilized centaur (half man, half horse).

Menelaus enters with the writing tablets, and the Old Man follows trying to reclaim them. As they argue, Agamemnon enters and rages at Menelaus for not letting him handle his own affairs; meanwhile Menelaus justifies his behavior by telling Agamemnon that "your thoughts are crooked, shifting with every moment" (332). Here Agamemnon's past and impending changes of mind and mood are metaphorically tied to the changing currents of Euripus. Agamemnon accuses Menelaus of directing his rage at the loss of his wife Helen toward an innocent girl and her father. Menelaus invokes the name of Greece and accuses Agamemnon of betraying his country.

A messenger delivers word that contrary to Agamemnon's orders, Clytemnestra has accompanied Iphigeneia to Aulis. Agamemnon agonizes over what to say to his wife and how to get her to leave. Then Menelaus comes to Agamemnon with a change of heart; he has taken pity on Agamemnon and will not allow his brother to sacrifice his daughter's life so he can win a woman back. But Agamemnon has changed his mind and is determined to go on with the sacrifice, fearing heavy retaliation by the Greek army if he refuses. A decision of such magnitude, when guided by *hamartia,* or mistaken judgment, is essential to the development of the classical tragic character.

When Iphigeneia and Clytemnestra reunite with Agamemnon, they speak happily of their love for him and the bright future of Iphigeneia; and Agamemnon speaks similarly of his daughter's future, but with the bittersweet knowledge that his daughter's future is a sacrificial death. This is known as tragic irony, in which "a character uses words that mean one thing to the speaker and those better acquainted with the real situation, especially when the character is about to become a tragic victim of fate" (*A Handbook to Literature* 523). As they speak of the sacrificial altar, the women have in mind a traditional offering to Artemis before marriage, while Agamemnon's reference to sacrifice has a much darker significance.

After Iphigeneia goes inside, Agamemnon attempts to convince Clytemnestra to go home, but she refuses. The chorus then sings about the prospect of doom and cynically doubts the miracle of Helen's birth by Leda and a metamorphosed Zeus. This choral interlude increases the pity and fear that have been aroused in the audience through the tragic irony of the previous scene.

Clytemnestra emerges from the tent to find Achilles. As she introduces herself and speaks of his upcoming marriage to her daughter, Achilles denies any knowledge of such an arrangement. Both are angry at being misled by Agamemnon, and even more outraged when the Old Man comes by to tell them that Agamemnon plans to sacrifice Iphigeneia. At Clytemnestra's supplication, Achilles agrees to help her save her daughter, though he wisely insists she try to reason with her husband before he takes any action.

Later, Agamemnon comes to Clytemnestra outside the tent and begins to talk of the marriage sacrifice. An appalled Clytemnestra brings her daughter out from the tent and the two confront him about his plans. Clytemnestra is furious, and refers to his former ill deeds: Agamemnon married her against her will after killing her former husband Tantalus and their baby and cozying up to her father Tyndareus. Despite all that, she has been a dutiful wife to him, but this recent affront has brought her to judge him harshly, since he is proposing to "pay for a bad woman with the life of a child" (1168–9). Like the currents of Euripus, Clytemnestra's demeanor toward her husband takes a different turn, as she shifts from acquiescence to confrontation. Iphigeneia can do no more than supplicate Agamemnon and play on his pity.

Agamemnon explains that he is powerless to stop the sacrifice because all of Greece depends on it and his countrymen will insist on it with force. After he leaves, Iphigeneia sings a song of her own woe, wishing her fortune were different and concluding that "We humans are mere creatures of a day, and full of suffering, / yes, full of suffering is our life" (1330–1). This sense that human beings are ultimately doomed is an essential feature of the tragic form.

Achilles enters, prepared to do battle with the entire army, who have threatened to stone him to death for trying to save Iphigeneia. But suddenly it seems that Iphigeneia's attitude has shifted. She is willing to sacrifice herself for the greater cause, saying "I should not be too much in love with life" (1385) and "It is better that one man see the light of day than any number of women" (1395); this is a stark contrast to her earlier supplication to Agamemnon, in which she says "The person who prays to die is mad. To live basely is better than to die nobly" (1251–2). Iphigeneia's heroism causes Achilles to fall in love with her and he is even more determined to save her. Iphigeneia bids goodbye to her mother and forbids her to mourn, then sings a song of farewell to life, into which the chorus interjects their praises.

Later a messenger arrives and relates to Clytemnestra the events of the sacrifice: when Agamemnon saw his daughter coming into the grove to be sacrificed, he covered his face with his robe and burst into tears; Iphigeneia proclaimed her willingness to be killed for the greater good of Greece; and as the seer Calchas performed the sacrifice, Iphigeneia's body was replaced by a deer, and she somehow disappeared to join the gods. The messenger concludes that "What the gods purpose cannot be foreseen by mortals. They save those they love" (1610–11).

Clytemnestra rejoices at the news but is skeptical of its truth until Agamemnon returns to confirm it. He suggests they be happy for their daughter's sake, tells her to return home, and bids her a buoyant farewell. Clytemnestra's answer is a chilling silence. ❀

List of Characters in
Iphigeneia at Aulis

Agamemnon is king of Argos and commander of the Greek army, who are set to besiege Troy, but cannot sail because of poor winds. When Agamemnon realizes that the only way to obtain divine help is to sacrifice his daughter Iphigeneia to the goddess Artemis, he sends for her under the ruse that she will marry Achilles. He changes his mind twice, first in favor of his daughter, then in favor of the fate of Greece, or so he says. The real reason for his decision to kill his daughter is unclear and a point of contention among critics. When Iphigeneia is sacrificed, Agamemnon is racked with guilt, but when she is saved and taken by the gods, he feels victorious and seems free of guilt.

The Old Man is Agamemnon's servant, given to him as part of Clytemnestra's dowry. When Agamemnon decides to murder Iphigeneia, the Old Man expresses his true loyalty, which is with Clytemnestra. He tells her of Agamemnon's plot, thus serving the function of turning the women against Agamemnon.

Menelaus is Agamemnon's brother, king of Sparta, and husband of Helen. At first he opposes Agamemnon's decision to save Iphigeneia from being sacrificed, but then takes pity on the girl and supports his brother in keeping her safe, only to find that Agamemnon has decided to sacrifice her anyway. Clytemnestra is the daughter of Leda and the wife of Agamemnon. Despite her husband's directions, she accompanies her daughter Iphigeneia to Aulis to participate in the supposed marriage ceremony. Agamemnon cannot persuade her to leave, and when she finds out that Agamemnon is planning to sacrifice her daughter, she turns on her husband, reminding him that he married her against her will after killing her former husband Tantalus and their baby. She is unwilling to stand by while he kills another of her offspring, so she enlists the help of Achilles, who has taken a liking to Iphigeneia. When she finds out that Iphigeneia was spared by the gods and taken away by them, she is coldly silent to Agamemnon. She has changed from a loving, ideal wife to someone who is potentially murderous.

Iphigeneia is the daughter of Agamemnon and Clytemnestra. She arrives at Aulis believing that she will be married, when Agamemnon has in fact sent for her to kill her. Her naïveté and romanticism make her a pitiable character, as when she gushes over the prospect of making a marriage sacrifice to Admetus when Agamemnon intends for Iphigeneia herself to be the sacrifice. She is also pitiable when, just as romantically she resolves to give her life for Greece. Despite the callousness and injustice that surround her, she maintains a kind of purity and thus is saved by the gods. Just before the knife falls, her body disappears and is replaced by a deer.

Achilles is a Greek hero and the leader of the Myrmidons. He is stunned to learn from Clytemnestra that he is the intended husband of Iphigeneia. Both realize they are mistaken, and when the Old Man tells them of Agamemnon's plans to kill Iphigeneia, Achilles agrees to help out of manly courtesy. When Iphigeneia announces that she is resolved to accept her fate and die for her country, Achilles' affection for her greatly increases and he is prepared to battle the whole Greek army himself to save her.

The Messenger from the retinue of Clytemnestra announces to Agamemnon the arrival of Iphigeneia and Clytemnestra to Aulis. He announces joyfully that "this day has dawned with the promise of happiness for the maiden," initiating the tragic irony that will come to its full intensity in the following scene.

The Messenger from the Greek army brings news of Iphigeneia's sacrifice to Clytemnestra. He relates that Iphigeneia's body sunk into the ground mysteriously and when the priest brought down the knife, it was a deer's body that became splattered with blood. As all violent action took place offstage in classical drama, messengers functioned to apprise the audience of action that they were not able to see.

The Chorus are all women of Chalcis in Euboea. Being young married women, they are aptly suited to observe the dramatic action with attentiveness and emotional intensity. They sing in praise of Greece and in sympathy for Iphigeneia. In a tragically ironic and emotional moment, the chorus sings "Great is the happiness of the great" (590–1) as Iphigeneia arrives at Aulis to be killed. ❀

Critical Views on
Iphigeneia at Aulis

GILBERT MURRAY ON THE PLAY AS TURNING POINT IN
THE HISTORY OF GREEK DRAMAS

[Gilbert Murray (1866–1957) was the regius professor of
Greek at Oxford and translator of numerous Greek
authors, including Euripides, Aeschylus, Sophocles, and
Aristophanes. His books include *History of Ancient Greek
Literature* (1897), *The Rise of the Greek Epic* (1907), *The
Classical Tradition in Poetry* (1927), and *Hellenism and the
Modern World* (1953). In this excerpt, Murray places the
play between the fifth-century tragic tradition and New
Comedy, praising it despite its incompleteness.]

But let us take first the *Iphigenia in Aulis*. It is a play full of problems.
We can make out that it was seriously incomplete at the poet's death
and was finished by another hand, presumably that of its producer.
Unfortunately we do not possess even that version in a complete
form. For the archetype of our manuscripts was at some time mutilated, and the present end of the play is a patent forgery. But if we
allow for these defects, the *Iphigenia in Aulis* is a unique and most
interesting example of a particular moment in the history of Greek
drama. It shows the turning-point between the old fifth-century
tragedy and the so-called New Comedy which, in the hands of
Menander, Philemon and others, dominated the stage of the fourth
and third centuries.

Euripides had united two tendencies: on the one hand he had
moved towards freedom in metre, realism in character-drawing,
variety and adventure in the realm of plot; on the other he had
strongly maintained the formal and musical character of the old
Dionysiac ritual, making full use of such conventions as the Prologue, the Epiphany, the traditional tragic diction, and above all the
Chorus. The New Comedy dropped the chorus, brought the diction
close to real life, broke up the stiff forms and revelled in romance,
variety, and adventure. Its characters ceased to be legendary Kings
and Queens; they became fictional characters from ordinary city life.

The *Iphigenîa in Aulis* shows an unfinished Euripidean tragedy, much in the manner of the *Orestes,* completed by a man of some genius whose true ideals were those of modernity and the New Comedy. Two openings of the play are preserved. One is the old stiff Euripidean prologue; the other a fine and vigorous scene of lyric dialogue, which must have suited the taste of the time far better, just as it suits our own. We have early in the play a Messenger; but instead of his entrance being formally prepared and announced in the Euripidean manner, he bursts on to the stage interrupting a speaker in the middle of a verse and the middle of a sentence. There are also peculiarities of metre, such as the elision of –ai, which are unheard of in tragic dialogue but regular in the more conversational style of the New Comedy. ⟨. . .⟩

There follows the inevitable scene in which mother and daughter—the latter inarticulate with tears—convict the father and appeal to him. A fine scene it is in which each character comes out clear, and through the still young and obedient Clytemnestra one descries the shadow of the great murderess to be. Agamemnon is broken but helpless. It is too late to go back.

The two women are left weeping at the door of the tent, when they hear a sound of tumult. It is Achilles, and men behind stoning him. Iphigenîa's first thought is to fly; she dare not look Achilles in the face. Yet she stays. Achilles enters. The whole truth has come out; the army clamours for the sacrifice and is furious against him. . . . Will not his own splendid Myrmidons protect him?—It is they who were the first to stone him! Nevertheless he will fight. He has his arms. Clytemnestra must fight too; cling to her daughter by main force when they come, as they presently will, to drag her to the altar. . . . 'Stay!' says Iphigenîa: Achilles must not die for her sake. What is her miserable life compared with his? One man who can fight for Hellas is worth ten thousand women, who can do nothing. Besides, she has been thinking it over; she has seen the great gathered army, ready to fight and die for a cause, and, like the Chorus, has fallen under the spell of it. She realizes that it lies with her, a weak girl, to help them to victory. All great Hellas is looking to her; and she is proud and glad to give her life for Hellas.—It is a beautiful and simple speech. And the pride of Achilles withers up before it. In a new tone he answers: 'God would indeed have made him blessed if he had won her for his wife. As it is, Iphigenîa is right. . . .' Yet he

offers still to fight for her and save her. She does not know what
death is; and he loves her.—She answers that her mind is made up.
'Do not die for me, but leave me to save Hellas, if I can.' Achilles
yields. Still he will go and stand beside the altar, armed; if at the last
moment she calls to him, he is ready. So he goes. The mother and
daughter bid one another a last farewell, and with a song of triumph
Iphigenîa, escorted by her maidens, goes forth to meet the slaugh-
terers. . . . Here the authentic part of our play begins to give out.
There are fragments of a messenger's speech afterwards, and it is
likely on the whole that Artemis saved the victim, as is assumed in
the other *Iphigenîa* play.

The *Iphigenîa in Aulis*, in spite of its good plot, is not really one of
Euripides' finest works; yet, if nothing else of his were preserved, it
would be enough to mark him out as a tremendous power in the
development of Greek literature. Readers who enjoy drama but have
never quite accustomed themselves to the stately conventions of
fifth-century tragedy very often like it better than any other Greek
play. It is curiously different from its twin sister the *Bacchae*.

—Gilbert Murray, *Euripides and His Age* (London: Oxford University
Press, 1965, first published 1918): pp. 87–88, 90–91.

JOHN FERGUSON ON IPHIGENEIA'S HEROISM

[John Ferguson's numerous works include *The Religions of
the Roman Empire* (1970), *The Heritage of Hellenism* (1973),
and *Among the Gods: An Archaeological Exploration of
Ancient Greek Religion* (1989). In this excerpt, Ferguson
praises the theatricality of the play and compares Iphigeneia's heroism to that of other Euripidean women.]

The sheer theatricality of the play is superb. It has a splendid
opening with the urgent message by night. It thus opens on the note
of hope, and thereafter fluctuates between hope and despair. As
Menelaus intercepts the message hope fades. Then in the quarrel
between the brothers we have continually the hope that Agamemnon
may persuade Menelaus. With the arrival of the Messenger hope

goes, and it is a brilliant stroke of drama to give it an illusory flicker as Menelaus is persuaded too late. Now comes the scene between Iphigeneia and her father, and hope soars as we see the love between them and sags as we find it to be ineffectual. The most that Agamemnon can do is to try to spare Clytemnestra—or himself—by sending her back to Argos. In this latter half of the scene, hope—but now in Agamemnon, directed to this limited end—rises again and falls. But hope is not extinguished on the deeper issue. From the confrontation of Achilles and Clytemnestra comes hope. Clytemnestra is to challenge Agamemnon. With Iphigeneia she does so, Agamemnon is inflexible, and hope changes to despair. Still there is Achilles; he will face the assembly; and again hope rises, and again it is dashed to the ground. Yet Achilles will fight; hope staggers manfully up; until Iphigeneia by her sacrifice puts the matter beyond hope and despair.

Iphigeneia then provides the solution, and in so doing she reasons in a way counter to everything Euripides stood for. He did not believe that one man is worthier than ten thousand women or that Asiatics are naturally slaves. Shades of Medea! This is no deathbed recantation of his life's work. It is tempting to suppose irony in view of the pretentious Hellenism of the Macedonian court. Yet Iphigeneia is no tongue-in-cheek creation. She goes on (1416–20):

> I say this with no—NO—reservations:
> Helen has done enough by her beauty to cause
> quarrels and bloodshed among men. Stranger—

she is addressing Achilles—

> do not die for me or put others to death.
> Let me save Greece if I may.

There is no irony there. Of course it is true that Iphigeneia is Agamemnon's child, physically and spiritually, and we may expect her to share his prejudices, and Euripides has prepared us for this. But there is more to it than that. What Euripides is doing is showing that a girl with all the prejudices of Athenian womanhood can still be a heroine. His most dominant women, Medea, Phaedra, Hecabe, all except the pathological Electra, have been non-Greek. Here is a typical Athenian woman, and she still dominates the scene. This is not Pericles' injunction to the women of Athens, that their greatest glory was to be least talked about by men for praise or blame (Thuc. 2.44); on the contrary, the note of glory in fame is sounded by the chorus (1504). But it is Periclean woman attaining a glory which prejudiced males arrogated to themselves.

—John Ferguson, "Iphigeneia at Aulis." *Transactions and Proceedings of the American Philological Association* 99 (1968): pp. 161–62.

PHILIP VELLACOTT ON THE PLAY AS A COMMENT ON WAR

[Philip Vellacott has translated the plays of Aeschylus, Euripides, Menander, and Theophrastus and is the author of *Sophocles and Oedipus: A Study of* Oedipus Tyrannus, *with a New Translation* (1971) and *The Logic of Tragedy: Morals and Integrity in Aeschylus' Oresteia* (1984). In this excerpt, Vellacott discusses the play as an ironic comment on the prevalence of deception in times of war.]

The story of the sacrifice of Iphigenia was very well known to the audience. But in this play, even more than is usual in Euripides, assumptions about what we are going to be given are misleading. That, in fact, is the play's chief comment on war: that in a war nothing is what it seems to be. For example, ever since Aeschylus' *Agamemnon* everyone had known that the expedition to Troy was held up at Aulis by a stormy wind from the north-east, which could only be stopped by sacrificing Iphigenia to Artemis. Many modern readers have tried to interpret this play—have tried to enjoy it—on that assumption. But, we are in fact told, first in the prologue and later by Achilles (9–11, 813), that there is hardly any wind at all. Yet the sacrifice is still demanded. Why? No explanation. Agamemnon tells us he is reversing his decision to send for Iphigenia. But Agamemnon knows exactly how many days it takes a horseman to ride from Aulis to Argos, and how long it takes a carriage to come back; and he has delayed sending his second message until it is probable that Iphigenia is on the point of arriving, when the decision will be taken out of his hands. Menelaus, again, is ruthless at first, and leads Agamemnon into a fine posture of righteousness, a protestation that he will not sacrifice his daughter, that the whole war is a piece of lunacy. Then Iphigenia arrives, and Agamemnon sheds tears. Menelaus softens: 'Compassion moves me for the unhappy girl,' he says; 'why don't we kill Calchas?'—and his brother, like a puppet on strings, now insists that the sacrifice is inevitable. What is shown here is a phenomenon only too familiar in our modern world: the fact that in a corrupt society a destructive pattern of events, once set in motion, advances automatically, fuelled by the self-interest of numerous individuals, towards its prepared conclusion, regardless of the presence or absence of any rational motive. So in this painfully realistic scene between Menelaus and Agamemnon (471–542), we cannot be sure that any word or gesture is what it seems to be. There is indeed a driving force behind what happens, but it only becomes evident later in the play: the mutinous army. It was the superstitious rabble of soldiers who, once the idea was leaked to them by Odysseus or Calchas (518, 524, 1361–2), insisted on the sacrifice (1346–52). This aspect of the familiar pious story was specifically put forward by the Elders of Argos in Aeschylus' *Agamemnon;* and here in *Iphigenia in Aulis* the talk between Agamemnon and his brother (471–515) is not the emotional and touching picture it has sometimes been taken for; rather it suggests a plain instance of the ritual dance of diplomacy, in which forms of words follow a pattern felt to be necessary. There is really no problem; Agamemnon yielded a long time ago; now the two progress by formal steps towards an accepted outcome.

When Achilles enters, he plays a different tune in the same key. He learns that Agamemnon had induced his wife to send his daughter to Aulis with the tale that she was to be married to him, Achilles, when in fact he was intending to cut her throat at the altar of Artemis. Achilles is outraged; cold-blooded ritual murder, we assume, stirs his horror. Not at all. 'Agamemnon ought to have asked my permission before using my name as a decoy. Of course I wouldn't have refused.' Two other figures of authority in the army are named, Odysseus and Calchas; the commander-in-chief knows that he can trust neither. All these characters were familiar to the audience from Homer, where, if they are not to be unreservedly admired, they can be moderately respected. What Euripides is showing in this play is what twenty-five years of war have taught him: the power that falsity has over truth; the commanders who cannot command, the reasons which are covers for real reasons, the loyalty which is expedient, the resolves which are provisional; the banner of freedom held aloft by men who know their own slavery and find 'freedom' a useful excuse for doing what they intend to do.

—Philip Vellacott, *Ironic Drama: A Study of Euripides' Method and Meaning* (Cambridge: Cambridge University Press, 1975): pp. 174–75.

HELENE P. FOLEY ON THE INTERTWINING SIGNIFICANCE OF MARRIAGE AND SACRIFICE

[Helene P. Foley is the author of *Ritual Irony: Poetry and Sacrifice in Euripides* (1985), *The Homeric Hymn to Demeter: Translation, Commentary, and Interpretive Essays* (1994) and *Female Acts in Greek Tragedy* (2001). In this excerpt, Foley argues that Iphigeneia's death, which merges the two rituals of marriage and sacrifice, dissolves the conflict between them.]

In the *Iphigeneia in Aulis* Euripides expands the motif of the voluntary sacrifice of an innocent youth for the benefit of family, city, or, as here, nation, to form the basis for and climax of an entire dramatic action. This expansion of the motif is only one of the unique features of the voluntary sacrificial action in the play. Iphigeneia dies not to save a threatened city or family but for a Panhellenic war which has not yet begun and apparently does not have to be undertaken. In Calchas' prophecy Artemis demands the sacrifice of Iphigeneia only *if* the expedition is to be undertaken. The cause for which the sacrifice is made, Helen and the Trojan war, is both in the poetic tradition prior to this play and in the play itself a consistently dubious one. It is uncertain whether the play closed with the substitution of a deer for Iphigeneia and an apparent translation of the girl to divine status reported by a messenger, with an appearance of Artemis on the machine to make the same point, or only with the assertion of Iphigeneia that she should not be mourned in the fashion traditional to other such sacrificial victims. In all three cases the play affirms a status for its heroine markedly different from her known predecessors.

The major difficulty for interpreters of the play is how to evaluate Iphigeneia's final idealistic conversion. On the one hand, we have the dubious cause for which the war is fought and the rhetoric and tone of the action prior to the final scenes: the ever-increasing lust (*érōs*) for violence (*éris*) in the Greek army, the vacillations and self-serving motives of Agamemnon and Menelaus as leaders of the expedition, the pomposity of the future war hero Achilles and the fiercely personal outlook of Clytemnestra. The heroine barely manages to escape the terrible involuntary death of her predecessor in Aeschylus' *Agamemnon* and a scapegoating by an enraged mob. On the other hand we find beautiful meditations on love and war, marriage and sacrifice, presented in the choral odes. Iphigeneia, as she explains and justifies her idealistic change of mind and accepts her sacrifice, appears to bridge the gap between the action and the lyrics. Is the ending, then, either ironic or a burst of pure and cleansing heroism, or both?

In the *Iphigeneia*, the structure of the play hangs on the performance of a sacrificial ritual which is disguised for a large part of the action as a fictitious marriage rite. Why does Euripides expand the two motifs of the sacrifice of Iphigeneia and her fictitious marriage with Achilles, both mere footnotes in the previous tradition, until they dominate the play? Why does he emphasize continually the homologies between the two rites? A close examination of this neglected aspect of the text offers a useful beginning for analysis and a way of exploring the difficult counterpoint between the choral lyrics and the development of the action, culminating in the sacrificial death of Iphigeneia. ⟨. . .⟩

In the beginning Agamemnon invents a false marriage in order to accomplish an involuntary and unpropitious sacrifice of his daughter. The early scenes, by playing on the formal similarities between the two rites, emphasize his cruel deception. The middle scenes, although they expose the fiction of the marriage, ironically make this fiction so real a possibility that the entire myth of the Trojan war stands in jeopardy. Achilles is about to subvert his talents to a private rather than a public cause. He envies Greece his bride (1406). In a final shift the false marriage becomes the basis for the resolution of the conflict and the return to the myth. Iphigeneia makes the sacrifice voluntary and propitious and psychologically acceptable to herself by visualizing it as marriage. If the final scenes are genuine, she tames unbridled *érōs* and *éris* and goes to her death untouched by hostile hands. Iphigeneia answers the question of the relation between herself and the corrupt Helen by making her act a sacrifice for marriage, a means of reconciling her parents, and of putting *érōs* back into its proper place. The *éris* of the army, which was exploding in *stásis* and an urge toward a ritual lynching, is redirected to war. As Plato claims (*Rep.* 470b), war is the opposite of *stásis*, internal violence such as we see in later scenes of the play, where Achilles' own Myrmidons are the first to turn against him when he attempts to defend Iphigeneia (1352 f.). By contrast, war channels internal violence outward by ritualizing and subduing it to serve an ostensibly rational cause. Iphigeneia's act thus resolves the conflict between civilized feeling and private interest, which would deny her death, and political reality, the conflict, in short, between marriage and sacrifice, through her extravagant merging of the two rituals. The reason for the repeated, ironic emphasis on ritual detail in the play now becomes clear; out of ironic disparity there emerges a desperate source of salvation. The restoration of sacrifice and marriage, rituals shared by all Greeks despite their political differences, is tantamount to a restoration and definition of Panhellenic culture.

—Helene P. Foley, "Marriage and Sacrifice in Euripides' *Iphigenia in Aulis.*" *Arethusa* 15 (1982): pp. 159–60, 165–66.

Dale Chant on the Role Inversions in the Play

[In this excerpt, Chant explores how characters such as Agamemnon, Menelaos, and Iphigenia vacillate between the roles of savior and destroyer.]

In the *Iphigeneia at Aulis* role and role inversion are paramount concerns. Indeed it could be contended that in this play we find Euripides' clearest and best defined account of human (and divine) variability. Agamemnon, Menelaos, Achilleus, Iphigeneia, and even, in the final analysis, Artemis, all take positions and attitudes diametrically opposed to those initially adopted. Moreover, the basic thrust behind these movements in position and attitude is the same for each of these characters. All are concerned, in one way or another, with the saving or destruction of Iphigeneia, a situation which most emphatically includes Iphigeneia herself. For on the one hand she wildly supplicates to be saved, while on the other she gladly offers her body to the blade. In addition, Iphigeneia plays a crucial role in greater destructions. If she is destroyed by Agamemnon's and the army's actions, then Greece is destroyed in turn by her (Agamemnon's and the Greeks' final triumph is a 'Pyrrhic' victory at best), a situation made all the more ironic by her affected stance of saviour to the fatherland. In Iphigeneia's case, however, the discrepancy between intention and the consequences of action is innocent enough. The play gives no hint that she is at all aware of the irony implicit in her actions. But such lack of awareness is not postulated with regard to Agamemnon, Menelaos and Achilleus. The duplicities and hypocrisies of these three have been the subject of much analysis, and it is at least a critical commonplace to observe that they are characterised in a way more reminiscent of the sour end of everyday life than of the due proprieties associated with heroic, or Homeric, behaviour.

The literary mechanism by which such characterisations are established is simple enough—duplicity and hypocrisy is indicated by the vacillations and reversals of adopted roles. But these vacillations and reversals function as part of a greater pattern of undermining and instability, of deception, seeming and uncertainty, all of which are factors which increase emphatically in significance as the play moves towards the exodos. Achilleus believes in his marriage with Iphigeneia; Iphigeneia believes, on the contrary, that she is marrying Hellas and Hades; the purported reality is that she is sacrificed, not married at all, yet the evidence for this—a messenger's narrative—raises serious questions about the ways in which an audience receives and interprets the facts of the play. Simply put, it is very difficult indeed to extrapolate from the messenger's narrative a viable interpretation of what finally happens to Iphigeneia. Is Artemis' role as arch-destroyer of Iphigeneia transmuted in the last instance to that of saviour, or does the context of undeniable vested interest bring pressure to bear upon any determinations an audience may care to make? My purpose in this study is to assess the movements of role among the various characters between the two polarities of saviour/destroyer, to relate that assessment to the increasingly revealed discrepancy between actuality and unreality, and to develop a reading of the exodus which takes these factors into account.

Agamemnon at the opening of the play is in a state of severe regret and indecision regarding his plans for his daughter. He has already sent a lying communication to his wife, telling her to send Iphigeneia to him, and is now breaking and resealing a counter-order, telling her to stay at home. Agamemnon finally decides to send the counter-order, but it is intercepted by Menelaos, who is, of course, very eager for the sacrifice to go ahead, since it will be the means by which he retrieves his wife. An *agon* follows in which Agamemnon and Menelaos exchange recriminations and insults, Agamemnon advocating his desire to save his daughter, and Menelaos claiming that he has now unjustifiably changed his mind—Agamemnon was previously glad of this opportunity to break the indefinite stay at Aulis—and that failure to sacrifice means dishonour for the Greeks, since they would then be allowing barbarians to steal their women with impunity. Agamemnon's role has at this point changed from that of ambitious general, willing to put military advancement above family affection, to that of caring father, willing to disband the fleet rather than destroy his own daughter. Menelaos' attitude has remained constant; but when after the *agon* Iphigeneia and Klytaimestra arrive, their arrival is the stimulus for a complete role interchange between Menelaos and Agamemnon. Agamemnon has become resigned to his daughter's fate and is now willing to go through with the sacrifice, but Menelaos, as if suddenly moved by pity, becomes Iphigeneia's advocate and now attempts to save her. The destroyer adopts the stance of the saviour; the saviour, that of the destroyer.

Such inversions may well be hypocritical, with Agamemnon and Menelaos playing a game of double-think, but it does not seem particularly important, for the actual arrival of Klytaimestra (unexpected) and of Iphigeneia in the Greek camp, together with the realisation that perhaps Kalchas, and certainly Odysseus, will tell the Greek army that their future depends on the death of Iphigeneia, bring it about that Menelaos and Agamemnon are both forced into the role of destroyers. They no longer have the power to play roles of any consequence. This does not prevent Agamemnon from reverting to the role of loving father, concerned for his daughter's marriage when they met face to face, but his dissembling does not long convince Klytaimestra, who has learnt the truth from Achilleus and the slave. Agamemnon is now forced to pay for his vacillations. Unsuccessful as saviour, he must now act out the role of destroyer, even though such a role no longer appears to accord with his intentions or desires.

The roles of saviour and destroyer derive their significance from the fact that all characters except Klytaimestra play one or the other or both at some stage of the play. The duplicities of the two brothers fall neatly into a schema of multiple perspectives of which the saving or destruction of Iphigeneia is the principal focus. Iphigeneia, however, is no mere passive pawn to the machinations of Agamemnon and Menelaos—she shows a strident will of her own, however diverse. With equal enthusiasm and passion Iphigeneia first pleads for salvation, and then for sacrifice, first is afraid of death, and then gladly embraces it. By doing so she functions herself in the saviour/destroyer schema as one of the agents of her (own) destruction.

—Dale Chant, "Role Inversion and Its Function in the *Iphigenia at Aulis*." *Ramus* 15, no. 2 (1986): pp. 83–85.

EDITH HALL ON DECISION-MAKING IN THE PLAY

[Edith Hall is the author of *Inventing the Barbarian: Greek Self-Definition Through Tragedy* (1989), has translated *Aeschylus'* Persians (1996), and is coeditor of *Medea in Performance 1500–2000* (2000). In this excerpt from her discussion of the play, Hall highlights Euripides' interest in depicting moral decisions made by individuals.]

From pious Abraham and his son Isaac to the tale of Jephthah's sacrifice of his only daughter in the *Book of Judges,* the motif of the child sacrificed to please divinity has taken various forms in Judaeo-Hellenic tradition. *Iphigenia at Aulis* is the most detailed and developed literary version of this archetypal myth, but also the one which most calls into question the motives and integrity of the sacrificing parent. One of the most shocking moments in Greek tragedy occurs at the point in *Iphigenia at Aulis* where Clytemnestra, the heroine's mother, is desperately trying to prevent her husband Agamemnon from carrying out the intended sacrifice. Clytemnestra opens her appeal with the information that Iphigenia is not the first child of hers whom Agamemnon has killed. Clytemnestra says that she married him against her will, after he murdered her first husband, Tantalus, and tore her baby from her breast to dash him to the ground.

In no other tragedian does this information appear: the effect of the nasty little secret which proves that Agamemnon has always been capable of slaughtering innocents in his own self-interest is therefore quite devastating. Euripides has turned a tragedy about Agamemnon's famous dilemma over Iphigenia into one incident in the life of a self-serving warlord guilty of previous atrocity. But Clytemnestra, in the past and currently a blameless victim of her husband's callousness, goes on in the same speech to imply that if Agamemnon kills Iphigenia he may himself be killed on his return from Troy—that is, she threatens Agamemnon with the plot of Aeschylus' *Agamemnon*. Even a virtuous and forgiving woman, it is suggested, can be transformed into a vindictive murderess under sufficient pressure. Indeed, almost all the characters are portrayed as strangely wedded to the past, from which they provide narratives to justify a present attitude or action or decision. Yet they also seem curiously conscious of their futures, or at least of the characters they later became according to the mythical and dramatic tradition—an 'intertextual' feature which lends this tragedy a distinctively 'modern' tone. The inclusion in the drama of the tiny baby Orestes, it could be argued, forces the audience to 'remember the future' even as it recalls these characters' past.[14]

Clytemnestra's future is suggested by her characterization in earlier tragedy, but for the male characters the text against which *Iphigenia at Aulis* works is, above all, the *Iliad*. The youthful and naive Achilles of Euripides, for example, is given a trial run at conceiving a great grudge against Agamemnon, a precursor of the 'wrath' which determines the plot of the *Iliad*, and the Argive king himself is shown vulnerable to the moral weakness and inconsistency which in epic mars his generalship at Troy. The psychological depth with which Euripides treats the familiar story thus makes *Iphigenia at Aulis* one of his most profound and tragic plays.

Euripides was fascinated by the factors which condition the moral choices made by individuals, and in his tragedies repeatedly explored the dangers inherent in precipitate and unconsidered decision-making. In *Hippolytus,* for example, the hero's death is caused by his father's hasty decision to curse and exile him without proper deliberation or due legal process. Athenian history provides several examples of similar decisions, especially in time of war: a notorious incident was the Athenian assembly's furious decision in 427 BCE summarily to execute all the male inhabitants of Mytilene, a decision they revoked the very next day after a 'sudden change of heart' (Thucydides 3.36). This resulted in a desperate race against time as one trireme chased another across the Aegean sea. *Iphigenia at Aulis* uses myth to stage a not dissimilar occasion during a military crisis when several members of the same family took and rescinded hasty decisions about the life of an innocent girl.

Aristotle notoriously complained about the 'inconsistent' characterization of Iphigenia, whose understandable rejection of the plan to sacrifice her is subsequently replaced by a passionate death-wish (*Poetics* 1454^{a}26). It has occasionally been proposed, in defence of Euripides, that Iphigenia's predicament has virtually driven her mad.[15] But Iphigenia is only imitating the male characters in her own play. Agamemnon has summoned her to be sacrificed, changes his mind at the beginning of the play, but is incapable of sticking to the better moral course when Iphigenia's arrival forces his hand: fear of his own army's reaction prevents him from rescinding the authorization of the sacrifice. Menelaus changes his mind no less dramatically, emotionally rejecting his earlier 'rational' view that Iphigenia's sacrifice was an unfortunate necessity when he sees his brother's distress. Even Achilles, who longs to prove his heroic stature and defend Iphigenia against the army, allows her to persuade him that she really wants to die. Is it so surprising that a young girl should be swayed by the militaristic ideology of the community in which she finds herself, when the strongest warriors in Greece are incapable of real moral reflection or maintaining a consistent moral position?

Notes

[14] C. A. E. Luschnig, 'Time and Memory in Euripides' *Iphigenia at Aulis*', *Ramus*, 11 (1982), 99–104.

[15] See e.g. H. Siegel, 'Self-delusion and the *volte-face* of Iphigenia in Euripides' *Iphigenia at Aulis*', *Hermes*, 108 (1980), 300–21.

—Edith Hall, "Introduction." *Euripides: Iphigenia Among the Taurians, Bacchae, Iphigenia at Aulis, Rhesus,* trans. James Morwood (Oxford: Oxford University Press, 1999): pp. xxii–xxiv.

Works by Euripides

Alcestis. ca. 438.

Medea. 431.

Children of Heracles. ca. 430.

Hippolytus. 428.

Andromache. ca. 425.

Hecuba. ca. 424.

Suppliant Women. ca. 423.

Electra. ca. 420.

Heracles. ca. 416.

Trojan Women. 415.

Iphigeneia Among the Taurians. ca. 414.

Ion. ca. 413.

Helen. 412.

Cyclops. ca. 412.

Phoenician Women. ca. 410.

Orestes. 408.

Bacchae. Performed posthumously.

Iphigeneia at Aulis. Performed posthumously.

Works About
Euripides

Appleton, R. B. *Euripides the Idealist.* London: J. M. Dent and Sons Ltd., 1927.

Bongie, Elizabeth Bryson. "Heroic Elements in the *Medea* of Euripides." *Transactions and Proceedings of the American Philological Association* 107 (1977): 27–56.

Bowersock, G. W., et al., eds. *Arktouros: Hellenic Studies Presented to Bernard M. W. Knox on the Occasion of his 65th Birthday.* Berlin: W. De Gruyter, 1979.

Burian, Peter. "Alcestis Resurrected." *The American Poetry Review* 5 (1976): 43–45.

———, ed. *Directions in Euripidean Criticism: A Collection of Essays.* Durham: Duke University Press, 1985.

Burnett, Anne Pippin. *Catastrophe Survived Euripides' Plays of Mixed Reversal.* Oxford: Clarendon Press, 1971.

———. "The Virtues of Admetus." *Classical Philology* 60 (1965): 240–255.

Buttrey, T. V. "Accident and Design in Euripides' *Medea.*" *American Journal of Philology* 79 (1958): 1–17.

Buxton, Richard. "News from Cithaeron: Narrators and Narratives in the *Bacchae.*" *Pallas* 90 (1970): 39–48.

Chant, Dale. "Role Inversion and Its Function in the *Iphigenia at Aulis.*" *Ramus* 15 (1986): 83–92.

Collard, Christopher. *Euripides.* Oxford: Published for the Classical Association at the Clarendon Press, 1981.

Conacher, D. J. *Euripidean Drama: Myth, Theme and Structure.* Toronto: University of Toronto Press, 1967.

Csapo, Eric, and William J. Slater. *The Context of Ancient Drama.* Ann Arbor: University of Michigan Press, 1995.

Davidson, Clifford, et al., eds. *Drama and the Classical Heritage: Comparative and Critical Essays.* New York: AMS Press, Inc., 1993.

Devereux, George. "The Psychotherapy Scene in Euripides' *Bacchae*." *Journal of Hellenistic Studies* 90 (1970): 35–48.

Dodds, E. R., ed. *Euripides' Bacchae*, 2ⁿᵈ edition. Oxford: Clarendon Press, 1960.

———. "Euripides the Irrationalist." *Classical Review* 43 (1929): 97–104.

Eisner, Robert. "Euripides' Use of Myth." *Arethusa* 12 (1979): 153–174.

Ferguson, John. "Iphigeneia at Aulis." *Transactions and Proceedings of the American Philological Association* 99 (1968): 157–163.

Foley, Helene P. "Marriage and Sacrifice in Euripides' *Iphigenia in Aulis*." *Arethusa* 15 (1982): 159–180.

———. "Medea's Divided Self." *Classical Antiquity* 8 (1989): 61–85.

———. *Ritual Irony: Poetry and Sacrifice in Euripides*. Ithaca: Cornell University Press, 1985.

Gillespie, Stuart, ed. *The Poets on the Classics: An Anthology of English Poets' Writings on the Classical Poets and Dramatists from Chaucer to the Present*. London: Routledge, 1988.

Goff, Barbara, ed. *History, Tragedy, Theory: Dialogues on Athenian Drama*. Austin: University of Texas Press, 1995.

Gounaridou, Kiki. *Euripides and Alcestis: Speculations, Simulations, and Stories of Love in the Athenian Culture*. Lanham, MD: University Press of America, 1998.

———. "The Simulation of the Statue in Euripides' *Alcestis*." *Text & Presentation: The Journal of the Comparative Drama Conference* 14 (1993): 47–50.

Gregory, Justina. "Euripides' *Alcestis*." *Hermes* 107 (1979): 259–270.

———. *Euripides and the Instruction of the Athenians*. Ann Arbor: University of Michigan Press, 1991.

Grube, G. M. A. *The Drama of Euripides*. London: Methuen & Co., Ltd., 1941.

Halleran, Michael. *Stagecraft in Euripides*. Totowa, NJ: Barnes and Noble, 1985.

Hourmoziades, Nicholaos C. *Production and Imagination in Euripides: Form and Function of the Scenic Space*. Athens: 1965.

Knox, Bernard. "The *Medea* of Euripides." *Yale Classical Studies* 25 (1977): 193–225.

———. *Word and Action: Essays on the Ancient Theater.* Baltimore: The Johns Hopkins University Press, 1979.

Kovacs, David. "On Medea's Great Monologue." *Classical Quarterly* 36 (1986): 343–352.

———. "Zeus in Euripides' *Medea.*" *American Journal of Philology* 114 (1993): 45–70.

Lefkowitz, Mary R. "'Impiety' and 'Atheism' in Euripides' Dramas." *The Classical Quarterly* 39 (1989): 70–82.

———. *The Lives of the Greek Poets.* London: Duckworth, 1981.

Leinieks, Valdis. *The City of Dionysus: A Study of Euripides' Bakchai.* Stuttgart: B. G. Teubner, 1996.

Loraux, Nicole. *Tragic Ways of Killing a Woman,* trans. Anthony Forster. Cambridge, MA: Harvard University Press, 1987.

Luschnig, C. A. E. "Time and Memory in Euripides' *Iphigenia at Aulis.*" *Ramus* 11 (1982): 99–104.

Mills, S. P. "The Sorrows of Medea." *Classical Philology* 75 (October 1980): 289–296.

Murray, Gilbert. *Euripides and His Age.* London: Oxford University Press, 1965. First published 1918.

Oranje, Hans. *Euripides' Bacchae: The Play and Its Audience.* Leiden: E. J. Brill, 1984.

Phelan, Virginia B. *Two Ways of Life and Death:* Alcestis *and* The Cocktail Party. New York: Garland, 1990.

Pickard-Cambridge, Arthur Wallace. *The Dramatic Festivals of Athens,* revised 2nd ed. Oxford: Clarendon Press, 1988.

———. *The Theatre of Dionysus in Athens.* Oxford: Clarendon Press, 1946.

Powell, Anton, ed. *Euripides, Women and Sexuality.* New York: Routledge, 1990.

Sale, William. *Existentialism and Euripides: Sickness, Tragedy and Divinity in the* Medea, *the* Hippolytus *and the* Bacchae. Victoria, Australia: Aureal Publications, 1977.

———. "The Psychoanalysis of Pentheus in the *Bacchae* of Euripides." *Yale Classical Studies* 21 (1972): 63–82.

Scott, William C. "Two Suns over Thebes: Imagery and Stage Effects in the *Bacchae*." *Transactions of the American Philological Association* 105 (1975): 333–346.

Segal, Charles. *Euripides and the Poetics of Sorrow: Art, Gender, and Commemoration in* Alcestis, Hippolytus, *and* Hecuba. Durham, NC: Duke University Press, 1993.

Segal, Erich, ed. *Greek Tragedy: Modern Essays in Criticism*. New York: Harper & Row, 1983.

———, ed. *Euripides: A Collection of Critical Essays*. Englewood Cliffs, NJ: Prentice-Hall, 1968.

Seidensticker, Bernd. "Comic Elements in Euripides' *Bacchae*." *American Journal of Philosophy* 99 (1978): 303–20.

Siegel, Herbert. "Self-Delusion and the *Volte-Face* of Iphigenia in Euripides' *Iphigenia at Aulis*." *Hermes* 108 (1980): 300–21.

———. "Agamemnon in Euripides' *Iphigenia at Aulis*." *Hermes* 109 (1981): 257–65.

Stevens, P. T. "Euripides and the Athenians." *Journal of Hellenic Studies* 76 (1956): 87–94.

Vellacott, Philip. *Ironic Drama: A Study of Euripides' Method and Meaning*. Cambridge: Cambridge University Press, 1975.

Verrall, A. W. *Euripides the Rationalist: A Study in the History of Art and Religion*. Cambridge: Cambridge University Press, 1895.

Whitehorne, John E. G. "The Dead as Spectacle in Euripides' *Bacchae* and *Supplices*." *Hermes* 114 (1986): 59–72.

Whitman, Cedric H. *Euripides and the Full Circle of Myth*. Cambridge, MA: Harvard University Press, 1974.

Wilson, Douglas B. "Euripides' *Alcestis* and the Ending of Shakespeare's *The Winter's Tale*." *Iowa State Journal of Research* 58 (1984): 345–355.

Winkler, John J., and Froma Zeitlin eds. *Nothing to Do with Dionysos?: Athenian Drama in Its Social Context*. Princeton, NJ: Princeton University Press, 1990.

Wycherley, R. E. "Aristophanes and Euripides." *Greece & Rome* 15 (1946): 98–107.

Acknowledgments

Reprinted by permission of the publisher from *Tragic Ways of Killing a Woman* by Nicole Loreaux, translated by Anthony Forster, pp. 26–29, Cambridge, Mass.: Harvard University Press, Copyright © 1987 by the President and Fellows of Harvard College.

"Machines for the Suppression of Time: Statues in *Suor Angelica, The Winters Tale, and Alcestis*" by Robert C. Ketterer from *Drama and the Classical Heritage: Comparative and Critical Essays* © 1993 by AMS Press, Inc. Reprinted by permission.

"The Psychoanalysis of Pentheus in the Bacchae of Euripides" by William Sale from *Yale Classical Studies* 21 © 1972 by Cambridge University Press. Reprinted by permission.

"The Dead as Spectacle in Euripides' 'Bacchae' and 'Supplices'" by John E. G. Whitehorne from *Hermes: Zeitschrift Für Klassische Philologie* 114 © 1986 John E. G. Whitehorne. Reprinted by permission.

"Translator's Preface" by Daniel Mark Epstein from *Euripides, 1: Medea, Hecuba, Andromache, The Bacchae* © 1998 by the University of Pennsylvania Press. Reprinted by permission.

Scott, William C. *Two Suns over Thebes: Imagery and Stage Effects in the Bacchae.* Transactions of American Philological Association 105 (1975), 343–346. © American Philological Association. Reprinted with permission of the Johns Hopkins University Press.

"Euripides' Alcestis" by Justina Gregory from *Hermes: Zeitschrift für klassische Philologie* 107 © 1979 Justina Gregory. Reprinted by permission.

From "Translator's Preface" by Eleanor Wilner in *Euripides I* edited by David R. Slavitt and Palmer Bovie. Copyright © 1998 by the University of Pennsylvania Press. Reprinted with permission.

Ferguson, John. *Iphigenia at Aulis.* Transactions of American Philological Association 99 (1968), 161–162. © American Philological Association. Reprinted with permission of the Johns Hopkins University Press.

"The Virtues of Admetus" by Anne Pippin Burnett from *Classical Philology* 60: 4 © 1965 by University of Chicago Press. Reprinted by permission.

Index of
Themes and Ideas